Born at Midnight

Born at Midnight

By
F. Peter Cotterell

MOODY PRESS
CHICAGO

© 1973 by

THE MOODY BIBLE INSTITUTE
OF CHICAGO

Library of Congress Catalog Card Number: 72-95029
ISBN: 0-8024-0889-3

Printed in the United States of America

Contents

Preface

I was asked to write a history of the development of the evangelical church in southern Ethiopia. One critic, at least, finds me guilty of being overly enthusiastic. But the story is one for which to thank God.

In 1927 most of the tribes of the vast area between Addis Ababa and the Kenya border were either Moslem or pagan. Dr. Lambie, onetime physician to Emperor Haile Sellassie, led the SIM into these southlands. For ten years the missionaries labored, and when the Italian invaders squeezed them out they left behind a handful of converts. Some five years later, when the Italians had been ejected and the mission again made contact with the south country they found perhaps ten thousand believers, worshiping in a completely indigenous church structure which has continued to fascinate and inspire all who have had the good fortune to experience it.

The book is the story of the early years of the mission pioneers, and that story offers an exhilarating glimpse of eternal purposes being effected through the history of kings and nations. And then we see how the fire spreads from province to province as ordinary people gossip the good news.

I have allowed the men involved to speak for themselves. I cannot speak for them. Every effort has been made to check at first hand each incident recorded. Hundreds of miles on foot, by mule, in Land Rover, and by plane lie behind this story. What emerges is the authentic voice of the church of southern Ethiopia, a church that was born at midnight.

I have not thought it reasonable to burden the reader with the complexities of a rigorous transcription of Amharic. I have merely tried to ensure that the reader would at least come close to the correct pronunciation of such Amharic words as I have had to employ.

Part I: The Catalyst
The SIM in Ethiopia
1927-1938

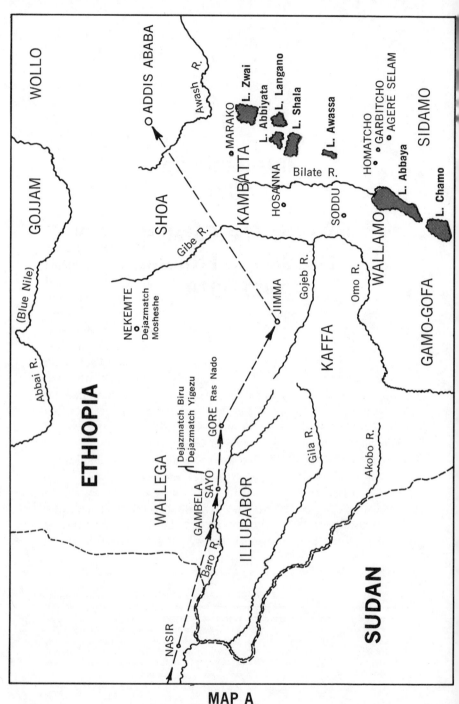

MAP A
DR. LAMBIE'S ROUTE TO ADDIS ABABA

1

Into Ethiopia
1927

On Christmas day in 1927 the first party of eleven SIM missionaries landed at Jibouti on the Red Sea coast. Dr. Thomas Lambie led the way; he had already spent seven years in Ethiopia and moved confidently amongst Somalis and Arabs, Amharas and Gallas. With him were his wife and his daughter, Betty. Mr. and Mrs. George Rhoad and their son George were there, too, formerly of the Africa Inland Mission in Kenya, and Rev. and Mrs. Rasmussen who had been with the Danish Mission in Aden. Rev. Walter Ohman from the United States and Clarence Duff, both new missionaries, together with Australian Glen Cain, who had joined the rest at Aden, completed the party. Left behind in England was Alfred Buxton, deeply involved in the new project, but appointed the SIM's home director for Britain with the task of advancing the work in Abyssinia in every possible way.

Dr. Thomas Lambie was a remarkable man: pioneer, builder of hospitals (two in Addis Ababa, one in Bethlehem), friend of high and low alike, indefatigable. In 1907 he joined the American United Presbyterian Mission and worked amongst Nuer and Shilluk at Nasir until 1919 when he and his family entered Ethiopia and opened the Presbyterian Mission's first station in Ethiopia at Sayo.

It was here that Lambie met Dejazmatch[1] Biru for the first

1. The many titles of the Ethiopian culture rarely have any precise equivalent outside the country. *Negus* is "king" and the emperor, *Negusse-negest,* is, literally, "king of the kings of Ethiopia." From the Amharic verb *zemmete,* meaning "to go on a military expedition," come the military titles *Dejazmatch,* "commander of the door." *Grazmatch,* "commander of the left flank" and *Qenyazmatch,* "commander of the right flank." Courtesy requires that the title *Ato* (an abbreviation or contraction of *Abeto*) should precede the name of a man, *Weyzero* that of a woman.

12 *Born at Midnight*

time. He was the adopted son of Emperor Menelik II and had recently been appointed governor of Wallega province. Biru plays an important part in the story of the early years of the SIM in Ethiopia, repeatedly appearing in the right place at the right time. But during the first three years that the Lambies spent in Ethiopia, Dejazmatch Biru fell from favor and was taken off to Addis Ababa, the capital, under arrest. Dejazmatch Yigezu took his place.

Among the people of Wallega province Dr. Lambie carried on an extensive practice. Many of the people he treated in those early days became his personal friends: men such as Dejazmatch Mosheshe, a district governor, and Ras Nadew Abba Wollo, governor of the neighboring Illubabor province.

Dr. Lambie must be allowed to tell his own story of his first meeting with Ras Nadew (Nado):

> We slept on the upstairs verandah of the house we were purchasing. One night we were awakened from a sound slumber by the sound of loud knocking on the outside gate. His Excellency Ras Nado, with fifty armed men, was announced and shown upstairs. In his sleep an insect had crawled into his ear and was causing him great pain. Fortunately I had an ear speculum and head mirror with me, and discovered a small black beetle, which I extricated without much difficulty and put into a small glass vial to let him examine it. He passed it to his soldiers who solemnly assured him that it was a wood-boring beetle, and that if the *hakim* [doctor] had not taken it out it would have bored through his head and killed him! I had to tell him that this was not true, but the soldiers inferred that although I might know how to take them out I certainly did not know the nature of the pest.
>
> He chose to believe them rather than me, and wrote a letter to the Regent, His Majesty Ras Tafari, saying that Dr. Lambie had saved his life, and a lot of other nonsense, which had the happy result of gaining us access to His Majesty a month later.[2]

Dr. Lambie made the long trip to Addis Ababa by way of Jimma, a rich coffee growing area, formerly part of the old Kaffa kingdom, inhabited mainly by Moslems.[3] During the long journey (map A) Lambie was preoccupied with two problems: how to

2. Thomas A. Lambie, *A Doctor's Great Commission*, p. 138.
3. G. W. B. Huntingford gives an interesting account of the Kaffa people and their customs in *The Galla of Ethiopia; The Kingdoms of Kaffa and Janjero.*

bridge the gap between himself and the regent, and what to do if he were offered alcohol. Lambie took total abstention seriously and he was well aware of the traditional use of the intermediary in meeting the aristocracy. Lambie was new to palace affairs and he wondered who his intermediary would be. This problem was at once settled for him when he entered the audience chamber in the palace in Addis Ababa, for there, seated beside the regent, was his old friend from Wallega, Dejazmatch Biru. And when the emperor offered refreshments, it was a tea trolley that the servants wheeled in.

At this meeting the regent proposed that the American mission should build a hospital for which he would grant the land. At later meetings details were agreed upon, and in 1921 Lambie left Ethiopia for America with the proposal in its final form and with a letter from the regent to President Harding of the United States. The next few months were spent in raising the finance for the new hospital. The mission, however, was unable to allocate funds for Lambie's project so, typically, he raised the money himself.

Early in 1922 Lambie was back in Ethiopia and construction of the new hospital[4] was soon under way at Gulele, to the north of the capital. Lambie was anxious to extend the work of the mission into the southern provinces, but the mission did not agree. Perplexed, Lambie pushed on with the building work until, with that task complete, in 1926 he again went on furlough.

It was at this point that his path crossed that of Alfred Buxton, son-in-law of C. T. Studd, who founded the Heart of Africa Mission. There had been repeated disagreements in HAM, and Buxton had worked as a mediator in the disputes. His health had suffered, so he and his wife, Edith, were going on furlough.

The American committee of HAM, led by Miss Constance Brandon, wrote to Buxton asking him if he could suggest some new area in which the discontented HAM missionaries might work independently of Studd. It was precisely then that Buxton's attention was drawn to an article by Dr. Lambie, published in the magazine *World Dominion,* and entitled "The Importance of Abyssinia." In the article Lambie had pointed to the arrival of Charles Bentinck, a well-known Christian layman as British minister in

---

4. The hospital has since been successively called Pasteur Institute and Central Medical Laboratory.

Addis Ababa, as a key to missionary work in Ethiopia. Now Mrs. Bentinck, later Lady Bentinck, was the sister of Thomas Fowell Buxton, Alfred's second cousin. What was more, Bentinck was then on leave in England. The two men met and Bentinck strongly advised Buxton to contact Dr. Lambie.

So Buxton wrote to Miss Brandon that the man to see was Lambie, and that he would himself come to the States to discuss the situation with her and with the HAM Committee. On board the ship which took him and his wife to New York, Buxton opened a letter from his father-in-law. Studd accused the couple of disloyalty and severed their connection with HAM. Edith Buxton says:

> The letter from father marked the midnight hour of Alfred's life. Separated from the people he loved, cut off from the work he wanted to do, broken in health, a lesser man would have turned to bitterness and disillusionment.
>
> Instead he turned his mind away from the hurt within him and gave his whole energies to accepting a new challenge. From this time, for the next ten years, he pioneered new territory for other missions to come in and take over. He returned once for furlough. He never settled down again to mission life on a station.[5]

In New York Buxton, Lambie and the HAM committee met and discussed the commencement of a work in Abyssinia. Before the second meeting the Buxtons went to visit the Lambies in their home in Baltimore, taking with them the Rev. and Mrs. George Rhoad who had been AIM missionaries in Kenya. The Rhoads were very willing to throw in their lot with the new project, but insisted that they would do so only if Lambie would leave the Presbyterian mission with which he had been associated for twenty years. The decision was not an easy one to make and yet the whole future work of these three men and of hundreds of others would depend upon it. Dr. Lambie was scheduled to announce his plans at a meeting with the HAM committee on the following Thursday. On Wednesday morning Lambie records that his attention was drawn in his morning devotions to Exodus 33:15, "If thy presence go not with me, carry us not up hence." That afternoon while visiting his

5. Edith Buxton, *Reluctant Missionary*. The final sentence quoted needs some qualification; from 1933-1936 Alfred Buxton was living in Addis Ababa, working with the Bible Churchmen's Missionary Society in charge of a Bible school in what was in all essentials a typical missionary station situation.

brother-in-law in Philadelphia, he picked up *Daily Light,* a book containing biblical passages on a given theme for each day of the year. For March 3 one of the selected verses was Exodus 33:15. Only an hour later his sister came in with a book she wished him to use in their family devotions that evening and she particularly drew his attention to Exodus 33:15. The following day Lambie incorporated the passage in the prayer he offered at the meeting with the committee. At the conclusion of the meeting both Buxton and Rhoad told him that independently each had had his attention drawn to the same passage.[6] Now confident that they were doing the right thing, the three men pressed on with their plans for entering Abyssinia.

A new mission was to be formed in association with the Worldwide Evangelization Crusade, WEC, which grew out of Studd's Heart of Africa Mission. The new organization would be called the Abyssinian Frontiers Mission. But things moved slowly. The HAM/WEC committee seemed able to do very little for the three men. Lambie was a missionary without a mission society, and conferences at which he spoke did not even offer to pay his expenses. Then, at Stony Brook, Long Island, Lambie met Rowland Bingham, general director of the SIM. And again it was apparent that this was no chance meeting.

Rowland Bingham, Thomas Kent and Walter Gowans had entered West Africa in 1893 as the pioneer party of the Sudan Interior Mission.[7] Their aim was summed up in the title of the mission: to abandon the coastlands which were already well-provided with missionaries, and to press on into the interior. Within a year Gowans and Kent were dead and Bingham, ill with malaria, was forced to return home. A second attempt also ended in failure, but Bingham persevered. The first station at Patigi was followed by others and applications to join the SIM began to come in from all over the world.

Late in 1926 Bingham paid an extended visit to Australia and New Zealand, speaking at missionary conventions. Branches of the SIM had been formed, and a steady flow of recruits for the work in Africa began. But to reach the work in Africa, recruits

6. Lambie, pp. 165-66.
7. *Sudan* is an anglicized form of the Arabic word for black and was used at the turn of the century to describe the whole belt of Africa south of the Sahara but north of the Bantu areas.

traveled to Britain, then had to transship and travel south again to
the West African ports. As Bingham traveled back to Canada, he
began to think of the possibility of opening a new work in East
Africa, particularly with the Australian and New Zealand candidates in mind. On board ship Bingham began to read SIM's magazine and found in one copy a notice inserted by his wife but prepared by Dr. Lambie, announcing the formation of the Abyssinian
Frontiers Mission.

So when the two men met at Stony Brook, they at once began
to discuss the possibility of a joint venture. At Canadian Keswick,
Buxton joined in the discussions; and in the autumn of 1927
matters were decided. The AFM would sever its links with
WEC and become associated with the SIM. Dr. Lambie would
head the new outreach into Abyssinia, with George Rhoad as his
deputy. Alfred Buxton would become home director for the SIM
in Britain.[8] Their goal was to attempt the evangelization of the
borderlands of Ethiopia, and the approach to these areas was to
be from both sides of the borders. Since the southern borders were
in mind, this would mean an approach both from northern Kenya,
where Rhoad had been working, and from southern Ethiopia. Buxton was particularly interested in the area around Lake Rudolf.

During the period of their association with WEC, a booklet,
Abyssinia, was written by Dr. Lambie and Alfred Buxton. On the
back cover was drawn a rough map of Ethiopia with an arrow
directed at what appears to be Jimma, although the place is not
named. This suggests that the missionaries aimed at using Jimma
as their first staging post on their journey south and agrees with
the proposals outlined by Dr. Lambie in his paper addressed to
the board members of the AFM which follows.

The Goals of the First Missionary Party
of the AFM to Enter Ethiopia

The following outline of operations for our first missionary
party may be taken as approximately the one that will be carried
out; it being understood that certain modifications may have to
be made at the time: not such as would change at all the purpose
or plans for this advance into the southern parts of Abyssinia,

8. For more detailed information on Alfred Buxton's later missionary
work see Norman Grubb's *Alfred Buxton* and *Once Caught, No Escape,*
and W. S. Hooten and J. Stafford-Wright's *The First Twenty-Five Years of
the Bible Churchmen's Missionary Society.*

N. Kongo (sic.), Lake Rudolph country and the Somalilands, but such as unforeseen circumstances might compel. It should be understood:

1. This is not an experimental expedition. Much is known about the countries mentioned and their tremendous needs, enough to warrant the sending out of hundreds of missionaries without ever crowding the great unreached areas, but,

2. The most strategic points for commencing a missionary campaign are not certainly known, and require a greater definition before a great number of missionaries are sent out, so as to avoid any overlapping, and that accessibility, receptivity by native peoples, densely populated areas, Mohamedan (sic.) advances and other compelling factors be thoroughly weighed.

3. Information can only be obtained by observation and study on the part of the members of the first group of missionaries as there are no reliable sources of information.

4. That this first expedition should not only be for the purpose of information by travel and study, but should be definitely committed to beginning one or two mission stations, so that the work might gain continuity, and by a practical beginning give a real evidence to the Abyssinian Government that we intend to carry on.

5. That due to the lack of any means of transportation beyond Addis Ababa, caused by lack of wagons or auto roads, and the rough description of much of the country, that mule transport will have to be relied upon for the purpose of getting the information indicated above and for the conveying of missionaries to their locations beyond Addis Ababa. That this transportation element will, until roads be built, be a matter of great importance to the mission, and will mean that, for a time at least, the location of mission stations should not be too widely separated as this would tremendously isolate the missionaries from each other and make extremely difficult the missions [mission's] providing such conveyances of person and goods as would seem incumbent.

Understanding the above five points we can understand that the undeveloped condition of the country and lack of rail, auto or wagon transport will make a certain difference in mission planning. Although fully recognizing this we also recognize that we consider our call to the regions beyond and should bend every effort to go as far into the regions where Christ has never been preached as is possible, trusting in Him alone who sends us.

The character of the undertaking, as well as the character of the country, determine to a great extent the equipment necessary. Getting as far as Addis Ababa is a matter of no great difficulty and no special equipment is necessary other than that for the ordinary European or American traveller; one goes by boat and rail the whole way. Hot days down the Red Sea or Jibouti will need summer clothes, but immediately Addis Ababa is reached the same clothing as is worn in America can be used. Riding clothes are almost essential in Addis Ababa as everyone goes about on horse-back or mule-back. Horses and mules are cheap in Abyssinia and, though not as good as in America, are still quite passable.

It will be necessary in Addis Ababa to establish contacts with the Abyssinian Government and its officials, and to purchase and hire mules and horses at a price of about $20 to $25 each, for journeying to the south of its frontiers and finding out where the densest areas of population are, where Mohamedan [sic] advance is most threatening, where slave raiding is most prevalent and where the people live who are most receptive to the gospel message, and from due consideration of these and many others, determine the strategic points. No one can get this information but the missionaries. There are no roads, only trails. Maps are inaccurate and often mere guesses. It is necessary to get definite information so as to build wisely for the future. One or two locations might be regarded from information on hand. It might be conceded that a receiving and forwarding base is needed at Addis Ababa. Banking can only be down [done] there. Post office facilities do not go beyond Addis Ababa. A real and vital connection is necessary with the central government and this entails a base at Addis Ababa where mission parties can be received and relayed on by mule caravan to the frontiers, where banking can be done for the outstation benefit, where supplies can be purchased and sent to the frontier stations, and where post be received and sent in by private runners at weekly intervals, and where government contacts can be taken care of. No definite mission work as such to be undertaken here, as the Swedish and American Missions both have stations here as well as the Adventists. A house be built or secured in Addis Ababa where such activities can be carried on and where, probably, a missionary of business training would reside and large enough to entertain the parties arriving or departing for any length of time from a day up to several months as might be necessary. This to cost about [no figure given].

This place should be established at once, although not, perhaps, in its permanent location. It should have rooms furnished by the mission for receiving missions parties and for receiving calls from Abyssinians, from petty officials to governors, and even the Prince [Ras Tafari]. It should be comfortable without ostentation; most of the furniture could be made or bought locally.

Inasmuch, however, as the work is in unknown areas and far distant from the capital, and as long journeys are necessary, it is most necessary that the mission equipment be provided accordingly. Each missionary should have saddle and bridle, riding clothes, tent, camp cot, bed, chair, table, three blankets, blanket pad, mosquito bar [net], sun helmet, plenty stout riding or walking shoes or boots, warm clothing, lantern, waterproof bags or boxes for clothes, supply of simple remedies, raincoat and such foods as cannot be found and are [sic] individual taste would require, understanding, of course, that it is possible and practical to live entirely off the country that is wonderfully fertile and has such a wealth of food-producing plants.

That beyond the individual requirements, that the mission should maintain a mule caravan, properly equipped with pack saddles, so as to convey the missionary and his personal effects to his destination, and to bring in periodically whatever may be deemed necessary to keep the missionary at work and in health and such comfort as is commensurate with good work and happiness. This mission pack train would be needed to carry such articles as were not personal effects, such as nails and builders' hardware, tools, medicine, etc., as will be needed for building and equipping the mission stations. Most of the buildings proper to be constructed of materials gathered on the spot.

Since so much depends upon keeping the roads open for the missionaries to get their supplies and post etc., it would seem wise not to have the stations separated by too great gaps, as if they were too far apart the difficulty of supplying them would be so very much increased, so perhaps the first station should not be more than one or two weeks caravan journey south of Addis Ababa. One or two most needy places are known at about these distances and could be, and most likely will be, selected for the first station or stations. Property should, if possible, be acquired at these places, and a mission building erected and the stations definitely possessed, and a man and wife, or more,

be located here even during this first season. That by the time
this has been undertaken that the Field Directors or Field Committee with information then gained, be able to definitely decide
(in connection with the Board) on two or more further locations
farther on, but in the same general direction, and that these be
taken up as money and men are provided as well. That, if
knowing of possible places, the Field Directors do not confine
themselves to three or four needy neighbourhoods, where the
beginnings are made, but during this first year or two do ac-
quire as much information about the whole project as would
enable them to outline the entering in of the fifty missionaries
asked for now, and for the many more it is confidently expected
will come in later.

The Directors can pursue their explorations and travel work
only in the dry season, from October or November till May and
must then retire to a more permanent camp, an already established station or to Addis Ababa for the dry [an obvious
error for rainy] season.

The opportunity of these many tribes, millions of people, is
so great as to be almost incapable of exaggeration. A policy of
magazining small mission stations in these unreached areas,
with such speed as may be possible, maintaining touch with these
stations, and endeavouring to keep them intensely evangelistic.
Schools and medical work not to be neglected but, for the first
at least, no great institutions be planned. The missionaries to
be comfortably housed at mission cost in houses of native
materials but of good construction, a cook stove and a bath
tub to be placed in these houses at mission cost as they add so
much to missionaries' comfort. All buildings, such as dispen-
saries, schools, as well as mission residences, to be erected from
mission funds using native materials. Carpenter tools be provided
at each mission station and builders' hardware. The mule train
be kept for reasons of economy, and a service established linking these stations (and) missionaries.[9]

The first party of missionaries was now almost ready to leave
for Abyssinia. Although the time was scarcely opportune for expansion of the SIM's work and allowances were already far behind, still Bingham felt that the new work must commence.[10] Rev.

9. Thomas A. Lambie, paper presented to AFM board members, June 27,
1927.
10. In the SIM the missionaries were not then and still are not promised
any fixed allowance. All money sent in for allowances is pooled and shared
equally.

Walter Ohman had been awaiting orders to sail for Nigeria, but Bingham asked him if he was willing to go, instead, to Abyssinia. He agreed. So also did Mr. Clarence Duff, a Presbyterian. Mr. and Mrs. Rasmussen, who had been missionaries with the Danish mission in Aden, would join the party at Liverpool; and Mr. Glen Cain from Australia would meet them at Aden. They entered Abyssinia in 1927. On December 26 they enjoyed a deferred Christmas dinner on Ethiopian soil.

The political history of the empire of Ethiopia[11] and the story of the growth of the church in Ethiopia are closely linked, particularly in the years before the occupation by Italy. In 1908 Emperor Menelik II[12] named his grandson, Lij Eyasu, as his successor. The father of the crown prince was Ras Mikael who had been forcibly converted from Islam to Christianity, so that it is not surprising that soon after his accession, Lij Eyasu reverted to Islam. He elevated his father to the dignified status of *Ras*. He even had a genealogy constructed for himself, showing his descent from the prophet. Doubtless he felt that there was sufficient Moslem strength in Ethiopia and in the neighboring countries, Somaliland and the Sudan, to enable him to end the Christian enclave in the Ethiopian highlands. He was to be proved wrong.

Dejazmatch Tafari Makonnen was then governor of Kaffa province, having been forced out of the strategic and predominantly Moslem Harar province by Lij Eyasu. Tafari could claim undoubted descent from Solomon through Sahle Selassie, the Showan king, Haile Melekot, and his father, Ras Makonnen. Lij Eyasu's steady drift to Islam was watched with deep concern by the leaders of the Ethiopian Orthodox church. At a meeting of the council of state in September 1916 Lij Eyasu was deposed and Menelik's daughter Zauditu was proclaimed empress. Tafari, raised to the rank of *Ras,* was named as regent. Then Lij Eyasu was excommunicated and the people of Ethiopia were absolved from their oath of allegiance to him. Ras Mikael, Lij Eyasu's father, marched on Addis Ababa but was defeated and captured. For some years more Lij Eyasu wandered in the north, but he was eventually captured and imprisoned. A successful plot freed him

11. *Ethiopia,* coming from two Greek words meaning "burnt face," is preferred to *Abyssinia.*
12. Menelik I was the legendary son of the Queen of Sheba and King Solomon. E. Ullendorff has summed up almost all that can be said about this legend in his book, *Ethiopia and the Bible.*

in 1932, but he was imprisoned again and died in captivity in 1935.

When the missionaries of the first SIM party came to Ethiopia, Zauditu—traditionalist, reactionary, staunch supporter of the Orthodox church—was empress. Progressive and innovative, Tafari Makonnen was regent. The missionaries settled into a house opposite the hospital Lambie had built in Gulele and began the interminable negotiations with the authorities, particularly with the authorities of the church, in an attempt to obtain permission to move south. The opposition of the church, on the surface directed against the missionaries, was also slanted against the regent, who was blamed by the priests for the delay in bringing a new patriarch from Alexandria to replace Abuna[13] Mattewos, who had died the previous year.

In the absence of the patriarch, the most influential of Ethiopian clergy, the head of the monastery at Debre Libanos, the *echege,* questioned the missionaries on their doctrine.[14] Dr. Lambie, Mr. Rasmussen and Mr. Rhoad presented their document to a gathering of fifty or more priests under the leadership of the echege, Gebre Menfes Qiddus. The argument developed along the lines of the tenets of the Orthodox church which the missionaries did not uphold, such as the need for fasting, beliefs about the canon, the place of baptism, mediation of angels, and the status of Mary. The discussions extended over several days[15] and at one point Dr. Lambie went to consult the British minister, C. H. Bentinck (later Lord Bentinck). It was from him that Lambie learned of the arrival in Addis Ababa of Dejazmatch Balcha Abba Nefso, governor-general of Sidamo province, with a following of "ten thousand or more men."[16]

A few days later Ras Kassa, guardian of the deposed former emperor, Lij Eyasu, also arrived, presumably to add the weight of his authority to one side or other. The fact that after the succession of Ras Tafari to the throne, Ras Kassa retained his posi-

13. *Abuna* is Ge'ez for "Our father."
14. The patriarch, being an expatriate, rarely knew much Amharic, so that although he was the titular head of the Ethiopian Orthodox church, in fact the *echege* held the power and usually knew it.
15. The information in this section is obtained from Dr. Lambie's own contemporary report to Rowland Bingham, the SIM general director.
16. Lambie gave this information to Bingham in a letter dated February 17, 1928.

tion as governor of Tigre province suggests that he supported the
Ras rather than Zauditu.

The situation in Addis Ababa was extremely tense. Bentinck
suggested to Lambie that the missionaries might attempt to enlist
the support of Ras Kassa in their discussions with the priests, but
the foreign minister, Bilaten Geta Hiruy Wolde-Selassie, advised
strongly against such a step. He advised the missionaries to do
nothing for a week. The political situation at the time was occupying the attention of Ras Tafari to the exclusion of everything else.

It is not clear precisely how a settlement was reached when the
regent confronted the empress and Dejazmatch Balcha. The traditional story[17] is that Ras Tafari invited Balcha to the palace.
Prudently Balcha took with him a personal bodyguard of six
hundred armed men. During the feast which followed, Balcha began to discuss the regent's policies, becoming increasingly more
hostile as the evening wore on. In the early hours of the morning
Balcha mounted his mule and rode back to where his army was
encamped, only to find the place practically deserted. While the
feast was in progress, Ras Tafari had sent his treasurer to Balcha's
men with sacks of Marie Therese silver dollars. He paid each
soldier ten dollars, and told the guards that they were no longer
needed and should return to their homes. Balcha was left with no
ally apart from the empress, who lacked any armed support. He
took refuge in a church building, but the regent had machine
guns set up around the building and Balcha surrendered. He was
imprisoned for two years, and then retired to a monastery, but he
returned to serve Ethiopia again at the time of the Italian invasion.
He was killed while manning a machine gun. The hospital near
Mai Chau Square in Addis Ababa was built with the proceeds of
his estate.

With the political issues resolved, the missionaries attempted to
settle their conflict with the priests. After four meetings the priests
reported that Lent was at hand and that it would not be possible

17. The story is queried by Ato Bairu Tafla in his article in the *Journal
of Ethiopian Studies,* 7, no. 2 (July 1969). The main facts, however, are not
in dispute: Balcha came to Addis Ababa with a large armed following
which was dispersed without fighting. Balcha himself was imprisoned. The
story of the feast at the palace and the strategem by which the soldiers was
dispersed is denied, but see the fuller accounts given by Christine Sandford
in *Ethiopia Under Haile Sellassie* and Richard Greenfield's discussion in
Ethiopia, a New Political History.

to hold further discussions until after the forty-day fast had been concluded. This would take them well into the rainy season which would make travel almost impossible for any large caravan. But Bilaten Geta Hiruy again intervened, providing the missionaries with a permit which gave them freedom to "take the air," but giving no specific permission to engage in missionary activity. He advised them not to ask for such a paper: obviously there was little hope that they would get it. On March 7, 1928 the party set off from Addis Ababa, heading for Jimma, leaving the Rasmussens behind to form a base party. Among the muleteers was a young man, Biru, who later became the charismatic leader of the church in Wallamo during the years of Italian occupation.

The party headed first for Marako, some four days easy ride from Addis Ababa. There an Armenian trader, Joseph Behesnilian, had a farm. His brother Simon had suggested that the missionaries might be able to open a school on his property. At Marako they discussed the idea, but came to no decision, and the party pressed on southward. After pausing for a day of prayer for guidance, they continued south. It was toward the end of the dry season, everything was burned brown and it was difficult to obtain fresh water for drinking. The mules, too, were a source of worry. In their anxiety to buy good mules, the inexperienced new missionaries had rejected those animals whose backs showed sores; unfortunately the animals they chose had no sores merely because they were untried. When the sores developed they simply would not heal. Unexpectedly a caravan of unladen mules caught up with the party, having disposed of their loads in Addis Ababa. So the missionaries hired the proven animals and continued the long trip to Jimma.

Both Walter Ohman and Glen Cain recall clearly that they lost the trail soon after leaving Addis Ababa, but Clarence Duff insists that the way was not lost, merely that the terrain forbade their crossing westward in the direction of Jimma, directing them inexorably toward Kambatta. Actually Jimma may be reached from the Addis Ababa-Marako-Kambatta route by turning westward at almost any point, but the problem of crossing the Omo gorge must eventually be faced.

As they neared Hosanna, the chief town of Kambatta, they were welcomed by a great crowd of warriors and people, and escorted to the governor's residence. There Dr. Lambie was astonished to find a former patient and friend of his from his days in Wallega province, Dejazmatch Mosheshe, godfather of Ras Tafari. Mosheshe informed Lambie that another of his former patients from Wallega was governor of the neighboring Wallamo district and so the caravan pushed on to Soddu, the district capital of Wallamo. At Soddu they were welcomed by Dejazmatch Yigezu, who had succeeded Biru as governor of Wallega, but had recently been transferred to Wallamo. He, too, welcomed the missionaries, assuring them that they might open a mission station at Soddu.

By this time the party had ceased to be concerned with Jimma. The rains had begun and the rivers which barred them from Kaffa province were in flood. But before finally settling anywhere, the missionaries decided to investigate the situation in Sidamo province east of Wallamo. Dejazmatch Balcha was, of course, in prison in the capital and when the missionaries reached Agere Selam, up in the mountains above the Rift Valley,[18] the new governor had not yet arrived. However one of his men, Fitawrari Atena Giorgis, was busy digging up Balcha's treasure:

> All his days were spent in counting Marie Therese thalers. He could do about 50,000 a day, and as this was twenty-five mule loads of silver he thought he was doing pretty well.[19]

While the missionaries awaited the arrival of the new governor, they traveled around the area looking for a possible mission site. Garbitcho seemed to be a suitable spot.

When the new governor-general arrived, to the astonishment of Dr. Lambie it was Dejazmatch Biru. He inspected the site at Garbitcho, a thousand feet below Agere Selam, but still much of the time up in the swirling clouds, and approved it, offering to arrange for the erection of some buildings on the site. And so the first party reached the end of their travels. They were assured of a welcome in three crucial areas. In each of these three districts there would one day be a great church planted. But it would not be planted without much opposition and strangely, much of this opposition would come from the Ethiopian Orthodox church.

18. The Rift Valley, a tremendous natural fault in the earth's surface, reaches down the Jordan Valley to the Red Sea, breaks in a V-shape at Aden, and one arm thrusts down through southern Ethiopia to Kenya and Uganda.
19. Lambie, p. 173.

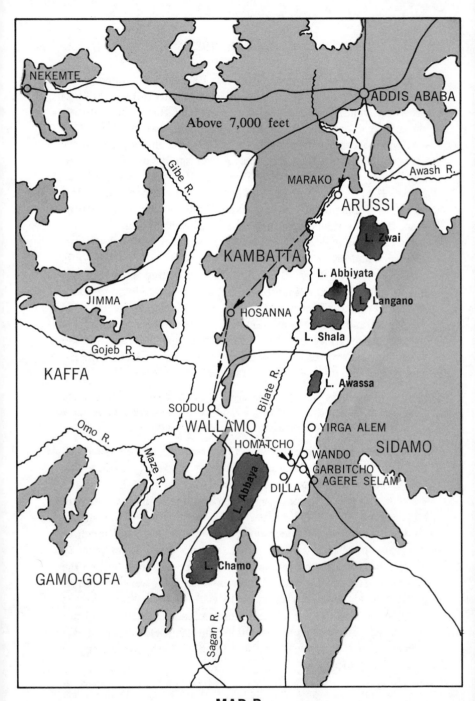

MAP B
SIM IN ETHIOPIA—1928

2

Roundabout
1928-29

The seven missionaries had now to make a decision about the opening of their work. At Agere Selam (map B), ten thousand feet above the Rift Valley, with the mists and clouds swirling about them, they met to plan the future. Glen Cain spoke first, expressing his conviction that he should remain in Sidamo. George Rhoad asked to be stationed at Wallamo, and requested that Ohman and Duff go with him. It was finally agreed that Dr. Lambie should travel back to Wallamo with the rest of the party, see them settled in there, and then return to Sidamo to rejoin his wife and daughter who would remain with Glen Cain. Tents were pitched for Mr. Cain and the Lambies at Garbitcho and then the rest set off on the return trip to Wallamo.

Betty Lambie was taken ill just after her father left, so her mother sent a messenger to bring him back. On the second day out the messenger reached him; at once he began to retrace his steps. After he had covered thirty miles, another messenger met him with the news that Betty seemed better and he should continue to Wallamo. When Dr. Lambie caught up with the others that evening, he had covered sixty miles in addition to the regular day's journey.

At Wallamo, Dejazmatch Yigezu told Lambie that he had chosen a suitable location for them, but the missionaries asked to be allowed to choose their own site. George Rhoad, who had experience in Kenya of the vital factors affecting the selection of a site, spent some time looking around the area. Eventually he chose a site running along the spine of a hill which was a continuation of Mount Damota, the most prominent landmark in Wallamo. The

27

site was not too far from the town. There were springs in the valley just below and a little uphill a stream offered the prospect of water for irrigation for the proposed mission station. When Mr. Rhoad went to report on their decision, the governor smiled at his enthusiasm and told him that he had selected the same site.

With the site approved and building well under way, Dr. Lambie returned to his family at Garbitcho. On his arrival he was pleased to find a large bamboo hut already completed, built in the local style. The hut meant much to the missionaries since in Garbitcho the rainy season lasts some ten months and life in a tent was misery. They soon settled down to the regular routine of language study.

They had scarcely begun to feel settled when they received a peremptory order from Biru to leave and return to Addis Ababa. Annoyingly, the governor did not give Lambie any hint as to the reason behind this unexpected volte-face. Dr. Lambie sent word across to Wallamo for George Rhoad to accompany him to Addis Ababa and Clarence Duff was to remain with Mr. Cain during his absence. Dr. Lambie and Mr. Rhoad went to see Dejazmatch Biru, but the interview was brief and stormy; all the governor's kindness seemed to have evaporated. Fortunately, a priest who had been friendly with Lambie in Wallega was at hand and was sufficiently distressed at the scene to intercede for them with Biru. With a quick return to that kindness which is so characteristic of the Ethiopian, Biru recalled them and gave them two or three months to obtain the necessary permits from the capital.

But in Addis Ababa the political situation was again strained. In September of 1928 was the palace plot; Ras Tafari was summoned to the palace by Empress Zauditu, apparently to face charges of attempting to depose her. As he entered the palace, the gates were closed behind him and machine guns, mounted within the palace grounds and on the roof of the great Menelik mausoleum, were trained on him. Rather than stay to discuss the situation, he left the palace and commanded the guards to open the gates. Overawed, they obeyed just as his own troops, alerted by his wife, began their advance on the palace. The palace guards were overcome and the whole plot was brought to an unexpected conclusion. On October 28 Ras Tafari was elevated to the dignity of king.

It was during the confusion of these months that the missionaries were ordered out of Sidamo. Although Lambie never was
able to discover the nature of the charges brought against them,
Mr. Cain suggests that it could well have been the Orthodox priests
near to Agere Selam who had complained about their activities
and perhaps threatened Dejazmatch Biru. When matters were
finally clarified, Biru did not permit them to remain at Garbitcho
but found them another location some miles to the west of Agere
Selam.

In mid-November of 1928 the position of the SIM was further
complicated by the arrival of the second party of missionaries.
With political affairs quieting down again and the king in the
ascendancy, Dr. Lambie decided to open two new stations, at
Marako and at Hosanna. Although he had been unable to resolve
the difficulty at Sidamo, he felt that he might return and explain
matters to Biru. He thus sent word down to Sidamo, asking
Clarence Duff to move across to Kambatta to meet the new party.
Syvilla Ferron was appointed secretary to the director, located at
Wallamo, along with Miss Bergsten and Miss Bray. Mr. and Mrs.
Lewis also were appointed to Wallamo, and Mr. and Mrs. Kirk
were to open the new work at Marako. A third small party arrived
from Australia and New Zealand: Eric Horn, who later married
Syvilla Ferron, was assigned to replace Duff at Garbitcho, Mr.
Barton was added to the new Marako work and Reginald Annan
went to assist Clarence Duff at Kambatta. Two days after Christmas in 1928 the group set out from Addis Ababa. Pausing only
briefly to locate the missionaries assigned to Marako, and taking
Mr. Kirk with them to assist temporarily in building the station
in Kambatta, the missionaries pressed on to Hosanna which they
reached on January 10, 1929. Shortly after their arrival, Duff rode
in from Garbitcho on his mule.

Mrs. Lambie was not well. While half the party set off for Wallamo, Dr. and Mrs. Lambie, with Miss Ferron, remained at Hosanna. A suitable site for the mission was found, and on January
22 Mrs. Lambie felt well enough to continue the journey. Scarcely
had they left Hosanna behind than a messenger came galloping after them with word that the owner of the property they had chosen, Fitawrari Wolde-Mikael, had ordered the three men off the
property. By the time that the messenger got back with Lambie's

advice, the Fitawrari's messengers had wearied of their wait and gone home. But two days later they were back again and threatened to pull down the tent if the three men didn't leave. The men met together for prayer inside the tent while the Fitawrari's men prowled grumblingly around outside. They soon grew tired of this and left, but of course the missionaries had no choice but to go. They packed up their gear and moved into Hosanna, into an unfinished house rented from an Indian trader, Pur Mohammed.

When Dr. Lambie reached Wallamo he discovered that the missionaries at Hosanna were not the only ones in trouble: the missionaries at Soddu had also been ordered to leave. Dr. Lambie with his sick wife, George Rhoad and their secretary, Syvilla Ferron, once again wearily turned their mules northward and set off for the capital. Hearing that Lambie was headed back to Addis Ababa, Mr. Kirk and Mr. Duff rode out from Hosanna to meet them; Kirk continued on with them to rejoin his family at Marako; and Duff returned to Hosanna where Reg Annan was stationed, prudently taking with him some of the food supplies carried by Dr. Lambie's party.

Back in Addis Ababa once more, Lambie felt himself very much unwanted. Pressure had once more built up against the king. There was a great deal of antiforeign feeling. On February 16, 1929 Lambie managed to obtain an interview with Bilaten Geta Hiruy who told him:

> There is a quite unprecedented uprising of the priests at the present time. In Kaffa province the Catholic Italian missionaries by unfair means secured six locations. When called upon to leave they brought suit against the Government through the Italian Legation for a large sum of money.[1]

A conference had been called to decide the status of foreigners in the light of the Kaffa incident; meanwhile the missionaries sat tight. At Soddu Mr. Ohman was ill and Mrs. Rhoad sent a telegram to the capital asking that they be allowed to stay until he was fit to travel. Fitawrari Negatu, acting governor there in the absence of Yigezu who had gone to the capital to take part in the

1. In his book, *A Doctor's Great Commission,* Dr. Lambie has confused the two trips to the capital, assigning the cause of the second trip to the first trip. The present account is culled from three reports circulated by Lambie to the missionaries in Ethiopia at the time of the second visit to Addis Ababa and a report on the situation addressed to Rowland Bingham.

conference, was unwilling to give permission on his own authority. Dejazmatch Yigezu agreed to Mrs Rhoad's request, however, and, in fact, Walter Ohman remained sick until Lambie was eventually granted the needed permit for the work at Soddu.

At Hosanna the position was very difficult. To obtain a little privacy in their tiny unfinished house, Annan and Duff pitched their tent in the living room. More serious was the fact that while Annan had a permit allowing him to remain in Kambatta for eight months, Duff had nothing. The days passed wearily. Duff eventually asked a lad named Ertiro if he would take him out to his home at Dubancho so that he might study the Gudeila language. Ertiro recalls that on his first visit, Duff unwittingly shared in a sacrifice to Satan as he held the ears of the lamb that was slaughtered for him. Ertiro was later given the appropriate nickname Ato Shigute which means "pistol" because he was so full of energy that he was like a loaded gun ready to go off.

On March 12 all foreigners were called to the shop of the Greek trader, Mr. Demetre, to show their permits. Duff had nothing to show and was recalled two weeks later and given five days to obtain a permit or else to leave. On the last appointed day it proved impossible to obtain mules and he was given an extension for two days.

In Sidamo, Cain and Horn had a trying experience. Dr. Lambie had been given two or three months to bring word from the capital. When in early March Biru discovered that they were still at Garbitcho and that no word had come from Lambie, he invited them to a farewell supper at his home and arranged for mules to take them to Addis Ababa. At first he planned to have the mission goods stockpiled at Garbitcho, then he changed his mind and provided the men with pack mules to take their goods to the capital. On March 4 they left Garbitcho. But they both felt certain that they would be returning to Sidamo. On the morning of their departure Glen Cain read 2 Samuel 7:10, "Moreover I will appoint a place for my people Israel, and will plant them, that they may dwell in a place of their own, and move no more; neither shall the children of wickedness afflict them any more, as beforetime."

Toward the end of March the two men arrived in Addis Ababa to find Dr. Lambie, George Rhoad and Mr. Rasmussen battling to obtain the necessary permits. Lambie was aware of the ex-

pulsion order served on Duff in Hosanna and time was pressing.
Lambie even spoke with Mr. Southard, the American minister in
Addis Ababa, stressing that the mission was not asking for political intervention, simply that Southard might assure the king that
the SIM was not involved in politics:

> The Field Executive Council felt that there was a danger of
> the Legation not understanding that our mission would not ap-
> peal for Government help or the redress of wrong either to them
> or the Abyssinian Government, that our reliance was upon
> God, and that in accordance with our constitution, although we
> made representations to them we sought no official action on
> our behalf.
>
> The FEC thought it advisable for this to be explained to
> Bilaten Geta Hiruy and the American Minister as well. Until the
> time we did this it seemed as if things got darker and darker, but
> when this information was given to them it really seemed as if
> God began to honour our faith in Him by putting a desire into
> their hearts to really help us.[2]

Negotiations were stalled again by the sickness of the foreign
minister, but eventually the permits began to come through. At
the end of March, Dejazmatch Yigezu told Dr. Lambie that he had
already sent instructions to Soddu granting the missionaries permission to stay. The details of the agreement proved more difficult
to settle. A document involving fifteen clauses was prepared, but
as the final draft was being drawn up, Lambie heard the governor
add a subclause to the thirteenth point: "They promise that they
will not teach religion." Although Yigezu assured Lambie that
this was inserted entirely for his own protection in dealing with
the priests, Lambie insisted that he could not sign the document
while the subclause remained. It was late. Both men were tired
and hungry but the scribe was ordered to rewrite paragraph thirteen, and this time the restrictive clause was omitted. George
Rhoad took charge of the precious document and returned with
it to Soddu.

On April Fools' Day a paper was received for Dejazmatch

2. From a report dated March 9, 1929 and circulated by Lambie to the
other missionaries in Ethiopia. The clarification of their position must have
come only just in time, for their visit to the American minister would at
once have been reported to the authorities who could only have viewed it
with extreme distrust in the light of the action of the Catholic missionaries.

Mosheshe at Hosanna, giving permission for the work there to
continue:

> Dr. Lambie's association has been permitted to build a hospi-
> tal[3] with their own money in Kambatta to cure the sick, there-
> fore do not prevent them.
> Further they intend to establish a school within the enclosure
> of the hospital, to teach languages and trades. Therefore you
> have been ordered to examine and watch them occasionally, that
> they may not teach other religious knowledge.
> Megabit 23, 1921 [April 1, 1929]
> Signed: Bilaten Geta Hiruy Wolde-Selassie

The letter was, of course, an instruction to the local governor
and not an agreement with the SIM. It was put into the hands of
a messenger and sent off at once to Kambatta, although the dead-
line set for Mr. Duff's departure was already past. The following
is a direct transcript of Mr. Duff's recorded account of what followed:

> On the Saturday morning all [Mr. Duff's] goods were packed,
> and the boxes and tent placed in front of the house ready for
> loading on the mules when they should come. Yet all the morn-
> ing we did not cease entreating God to bring about a deliver-
> ance, believing that He was abundantly able to keep us both
> here if that was His will.
> At noon we were eating what seemed likely to be our last
> meal together, for some months at least, when there was a com-
> motion at the gate, and the boys reported the arrival of a
> Fitawrari with a lot of men. We supposed he had been sent to
> see why Duff had not yet gone, but his tone, and the nature
> of his preamble, indicated a different sort of errand. It de-
> veloped that that very morning a telephone message had come
> from the Government in Addis Ababa to the effect that we
> were to be allowed to remain and work in Kambatta province.

It is not entirely clear how Duff received his reprieve. Dr.
Lambie's report is dated April 2 and makes it clear that on the
first he had been shown for the first time the rough draft of the
above letter. He also stated that the letter was to be sent early on

---

3. Through the years since that time the SIM has repeatedly been reminded of their responsibility to build a hospital. One was eventually built
at Leimo near Hosanna and opened in 1954. Local pressure on this subject
almost certainly is to be traced to this letter.

the third, Wednesday. It could thus have reached Hosanna on Saturday the sixth. But Duff's expulsion order, even when extended, took him only to Saturday March 30th. It seems unlikely, but possible, that the government should trouble to telegraph the information to Hosanna before disclosing it to Lambie. More probable is the suggestion that Duff managed to hold out for one more week and that he was mistaken in assuming that the permission had come by telephone.

The Sidamo situation had yet to be resolved. Biru was not in the capital and this meant that the direct intervention of the regent would be necessary. The weeks passed with the king occupied with very much more serious matters. Dr. Lambie's appointments with him proved abortive; an appointment would be made, and then broken. A final appointment for a Sunday afternoon was changed to the evening, to coincide with a feast and general entertainment. Lambie declined to attend. On Tuesday Mrs. Lambie was due to leave for the States for medical attention. Her husband accompanied her as far as Jibouti and then returned to the capital to finalize plans for the return south. Dr. Lambie's caravan set off while he had a final interview with Bilaten Geta Hiruy.

The minister rebuked Lambie for breaking his appointment, but insisted that he must, in any event, see the king before he left the capital. The following afternoon the interview took place, and a letter concerning the situation in Sidamo was promised. Dr. Lambie recalls a remarkably prescient statement by the king at that time:

> Do not be angry with me, nor think that I am unwilling to help you. You do not know what enemies I have. Do not ask too much of me for the period of one year, after which I will be in a position to do more for you.[4]

The interview between the king and Dr. Lambie took place in April 1929. Almost exactly a year later, on April 2, 1930, the patriarch publicly proclaimed Tafari Makonnen Emperor of Ethiopia.

Dr. Lambie left Addis Ababa the day after his interview with the king to catch up with his caravan which was already seventy-five miles south of the capital. The letter from the regent con-

4. Thomas A. Lambie, *A Doctor's Great Commission*, p. 181.

cerning the situation in Sidamo was to be sent on to them. A week later it arrived, left unsealed so that they might read the contents. The missionaries read it with growing dismay; it appeared to them to say nothing particularly helpful. But while Dr. Lambie felt that the letter would prove useless, Eric Horn persisted in his belief that Biru would permit them to stay in Sidamo. The party moved on to Kambatta where the authorities had refused to do anything about land for the mission until Dr. Lambie himself arrived. They reached Hosanna on June 13; a few days later George Rhoad and Glen Cain came in from Soddu, to assist in the selection of the mission site. Cain had been down in Soddu for some months, studying language, but he had been looking forward to the return to Sidamo.

The search for a suitable spot took many days, but eventually Rhoad was satisfied. Again transcribing from Mr. Duff's tape:

> The morning of the day Lambuda was discovered, a number of our party, unknown to each other, had been praying very definitely that God might no longer keep hidden from us His will, but might that very day lead us in some way to the place of His choice.

Fitawrari Zelleke had been appointed by the governor to assist in the negotiations, but even so it was some six weeks before they were finalized. Leaving Duff and Annan settled into their new location, Dr. Lambie and Mr. Rhoad took Glen Cain and Eric Horn across to Sidamo. They reached Agere Selam, "Land of Peace," capital of Sidamo province, on August 27 and were warmly welcomed by the governor. On the first evening there was a feast in their honor and on the second evening they entertained the governor for dinner. At their third encounter they presented their letter, the two leaders dubious, Cain and Horn quietly confident:

> Armed with the letter we approached His Excellency, seated on his velvet throne cushions. When he saw the Royal Seal he stood up, as all must do in reading a letter from the Empress or Regent, and bowed to it. He opened it and read it rapidly, while a smile spread over his face. Evidently he could read between the lines, and what we thought was a very poor attempt he considered excellent.
>
> "That is a very good letter," he commented. "It's all right now. Your missionaries can stay here. I never wanted to expel

them; now it is all right. How many missionaries would you
like to place in Sidamo?"[5]

The former site at Garbitcho was abandoned and George
Rhoad, guided by Ato Ganame Unde, who was to be associated
with the SIM in Sidamo for more than forty years, selected Homatcho as the new location, at a much lower altitude than Garbitcho and some miles to the west. Biru also had decided on a
move: Agere Selam was too high, too wet, and too cold, and he
asked Lambie to assist in the selection of a new site for the provincial capital. Lambie, guided as always by a Bible verse, took
Deuteronomy 2:3: "Ye have compassed this mountain long
enough: turn you northwards." He abandoned the mountains and
quartered the area to the north, and east of the Addis Ababa to Kenya trail. Yirga Alem, "May the world stand firm," for many years
the Sidamo provincial capital, until replaced by Awassa, was eventually built near the site selected by Lambie and Rhoad. At the same
time the two men also picked out a possible site for a mission
station if the new capital should become a reality. Lambie never
missed an opportunity for advance planning!

The SIM had been in Ethiopia for just two action-packed years.
At Soddu Dr. Lambie took up his residence with only Bill, his
bulldog, for company: his wife was still in the States having medical attention. Mr. and Mrs. Rhoad were there also with their secretary Syvilla Ferron. Walter Ohman, from the pioneer party, and
Miss Bergsten, Miss Bray and the Lewises, all from the second
party, completed the Soddu staff. At Homatcho Glen Cain and
Eric Horn settled in, with 2 Samuel 7:10 prominently displayed
on the wall of their home to remind them of the events of the
year past. In Kambatta district Reg Annan, who had been seriously
ill with pneumonia, and Clarence Duff were living at Lambuda.
The base in Addis Ababa was still staffed by the Rasmussens,
augmented temporarily by Elsie Downey, Mary Orme, and Laurie
Davison who arrived in Ethiopia toward the end of the year. Mr.
Roke, who had traveled with them, was sent down to join Charles
Barton and the Kirks at Marako. Twenty-two missionaries on five
mission stations were the visible measure of two years of hard
work.

5. Ibid., pp. 182-83.

3
Digging In
1930

In the late summer of 1929 Dr. Bingham escorted a large party of new missionaries to Nigeria, and wrote to Dr. Lambie and Mr. Rhoad that he proposed traveling by land across Africa to visit Ethiopia. They were to meet him in Moyale, on the Kenya border. On January 24, 1930 Dr. Lambie and the Rhoads, together with their son George, set off to meet the general director. They reached Moyale on March 1, but had to wait three weeks for Dr. Bingham's arrival. On April 16 Bingham reached Homatcho, the first SIM station he visited in Ethiopia. Three huts were already up; Cain and Horn were engrossed in language study. Staying only overnight, the party, with Cain and Horn added to it, pressed on to Soddu, where a mission conference had been arranged.

Apart from Mr. Ohman, who had gone to Addis Ababa to meet his fiancée, Marcella Scholl, all the missionaries from Wallamo, Sidamo and Kambatta attended the conference. A similar meeting had been held the previous year at Miango, Nigeria and a number of decisions were made which affected the entire mission; these decisions had now to be reported to the missionaries in Ethiopia. On Monday, April 21 the Soddu conference began.

Finance came first. The policy still held by the mission today was approved: the fullest information concerning financial needs might be given, but no appeal for funds was to be made. At meetings organized by churches at home no request for the collections would be made, although a "free-will offering" could be accepted. This meant simply that the usual church offering would not be looked upon as by rights belonging to the mission, but if a special offering, designated for the mission were taken up, this could be accepted. Financial needs of the work were to be made known only after approval by the district superintendent or field director. Missionary allowances, which had been biased in favor of the workers in Ethiopia to assist them in establishing the work, were to be equalized. The missionaries agreed to take up an offering to be sent to the workers in Nigeria to express their appreciation of the self-denial of their colleagues in West Africa who had willingly gone short to promote the work in the east. There was a sense of history in the making as Dr. Bingham handed to Dr. Lambie the first contribution from a church in West Africa for the Ethiopia project, an offering not from SIM missionaries but from the Nigerian believers in an SIM-related church.

Furloughs were also discussed. Four or five years was approved as a suitable first term, with five or six years for subsequent terms. Actually the majority of the missionaries in Ethiopia at that time completed six years or even longer before taking a furlough. Clarence Duff eventually went on furlough in June 1935 after serving for seven and a half years: and then he took only a truncated three-month furlough.

The question of the marriage of missionaries came up. Before marriage could be approved, both missionaries must complete one year in the country, and generally fulfill the conditions for appointment as junior missionaries.[1]

Polygamy has not been a great problem in Ethiopia, although involved cases of divorce and remarriage have occupied the ingenuity of the church elders and missionaries for hours at a time. The passage of the report referring to the SIM's policy on polygamy is striking:

> Relative to the subject of polygamy, Mr. Bingham cited the CMS,[2] who would not receive for baptism any man with more than one wife, and the CIM,[3] whose policy it was to allow a man who practiced polygamy to keep his wives when he was converted and desired baptism, as to release them often meant that they were then given over to lives of immorality, but the man must understand that if he incurs any new relationship in that sphere he will be put out of the church. The opinion of the

1. The general council of the SIM eventually abolished the hierarchy of probationer, junior missionary and senior missionary in 1967.
2. Church Missionary Society, an Anglican mission.
3. The China Inland Mission, later the Overseas Missionary Fellowship.

Home Council of the SIM was that they saw no scriptural grounds for refusing fellowship to any man or woman who showed real work of regeneration, and who was willing to follow the commands of Christ as he or she had light, and that the conscience of the individual missionary should be left free in the matter of baptism of polygamists. All this bearing in mind the Scripture that the bishop shall be the husband of one wife. It is to be hoped that the man will make Christian adjustments as soon as he is able with regard to the woman, and to the customs and practices of the country. The general feeling of the missionaries is opposed to polygamy.[4]

Brief statements on slavery and on the Ethiopian Orthodox church followed.

Relative to the question of slavery, we recognize that Christianity banishes slavery, but it does it by getting people in right relationship to God, and then into right relationship to their fellow men.

4. SIM, Abyssinian Frontiers Mission Branch, "Conference Minutes," p. 4.

Procession from the Abyssinian Coptic Church

With regard to our relationship to the Abyssinian Coptic
Church our position is that we undertake that we will not speak
against the church—that our work will be positive and not
negative. We will endeavor to speak the truth in love.[5]

The statement on slavery can only be described as disappoint-
ing, particularly when compared with the enlightened attitude to
the problem of polygamy. This reactionary response is all the
more surprising when it is realized that Tafari Makonnen was
committed to the abolition of slavery in the country.

While the missionaries had been traveling up from Kenya with
Dr. Bingham events in the capital had been moving to a climax
of which they knew nothing until their journey on to Addis Ababa
was almost completed. Ras Gugsa Wolle was a former husband of
Empress Zauditu and was dedicated to the overthrow of the
regent. He had been appointed governor-general of Gondar and
Begemdir. In March 1930 he marched on Shoa, and on the last
day of the month was engaged by Ras Tafari's forces led by Dejazmatch Mulugeta and supported by aircraft flown by two French-
men. Ras Gugsa was killed in the fighting and organized opposition to the king came to an end. On April 1 the Empress Zauditu
succumbed to the diabetes from which she had suffered for many
years.[6] On April 2 Tafari was proclaimed Emperor, and took as
his throne name his baptismal name, Haile Sellassie.[7]

These tremendous events were still unknown to the missionaries
as they prepared to leave Soddu for Addis Ababa. Bingham had

5. Ibid. One other matter was reported to the conference: the dismissal
of the Liverpool Council. Friction between the council and Dr. Bingham
extended over a considerable period of time. The situation was not helped
by the treasurer who, in 1928, had apparently misapplied some SIM funds.
Nor was the council entirely happy with Bingham's nomination of Alfred
Buxton as home director. Mr. Watson voted against the appointment.
When subsequently Mr. Watson was nominated by the council for the
position of secretary-treasurer, Bingham rejected the nomination.
   A rash of resignations followed. The council was dissolved on December
7, 1928 and business was carried on in the interim period by three council
members. No new council was formed until October 1930 ("Conference
Minutes" p. 3; "Liverpool Council Minutes").
   6. Rumors still circulate in Addis Ababa forty years later that Dr. Lambie poisoned Empress Zauditu. Lambie was away from the capital from
January 24 to May 12; the empress died on April 1 or 2 when Lambie was
still in the region of the Kenya border.
   7. His given name means "the power of the Trinity." It is as wrong to
refer to the emperor as Sellassie as it is to speak of the capital as Addis.
The capital is Addis Ababa, which means "new flower."

advised Dr. Lambie that it would be best if the SIM administration were carried on from the capital. Lambie himself was intending to join his wife in America where she was recuperating from her prolonged illness, so George Rhoad and his wife, together with the directors' secretary, Miss Ferron, determined to travel with the general director to Addis Ababa. On Tuesday April 29 the party set off. Reg Annan went ahead since Mr. Bingham planned on a brief visit to Lambuda. On Thursday the cavalcade met Walter Ohman on his way back to Soddu after welcoming his fiancée, Marcella Scholl, to Ethiopia. They discussed the various decisions of the conference with him and the next day he continued on his way to Soddu. Dr. Lambie and the general director went with Clarence Duff to Lambuda, all four men returning the next day, as Duff and Annan had determined on one more weekend of fellowship with the rest before returning to Lambuda.

On May 7 the party reached Marako, where Dr. Lambie was able to finalize the rent agreement for the mission property, and then to share in the discussion of the Soddu conference decisions with the missionaries there. On the final stretch of the long journey to Addis Ababa the missionaries met scattered groups of soldiers traveling back to the south after the fighting against Ras Gugsa. From Fitawrari Zemi, whose home in Wallamo had been visited by Miss Ferron, they learned of the events of the past six weeks. And finally, on May 12 they reached Addis Ababa.

There the situation was transformed. All opposition to Haile Sellassie was disarmed. The empress was dead. Ras Gugsa was gone. Earlier in the year Cyril had arrived from Alexandria as the new patriarch of Ethiopia, so the criticism from the ecclesiastical side was stilled. Although it was to be some time before Bingham would be able to obtain an audience with the Emperor, the future seemed very much more stable. Meanwhile, the mission pressed on with their original plans for a work in Jimma, target of their first expedition. On his journey from Sayo to Addis Ababa back in 1920, Dr. Lambie had traveled by way of Jimma and had marked it down for mission outreach. Now, with Dr. Bingham's help, a mission site at Qochi, in Jimma, with buildings and trees intact, was purchased from some Armenian coffee merchants.

May 24 was an outstanding day. The rest of the missionaries

in Addis Ababa watched what they called the "procession of the royal cats." Dr. Bingham and Dr. Lambie went to the palace to present to the Emperor two Persian cats which Miss Scholl had brought with her on the boat from England. In addition to the audience with the Emperor there were also conferences that day with the governors of Kambatta, Wallamo and Sidamo, where Mosheshe, Yigezu and Biru were still in power. The next day Bingham and Lambie left for America, leaving George Rhoad behind as acting field director.

During his stay in Ethiopia, Bingham had been made aware of some undercurrents among the missionaries: there had been disagreements between Lambie and George Rhoad, and some of the missionaries had tended to take sides. There was criticism of mission policy: some of the younger men had very different ideas from those of the more experienced leaders. After leaving Ethiopia Bingham wrote to the missionaries there:

> But let us not be concerned about our methods until, by thorough mastery of the language first, and then, through that channel, a careful entering into the thought of the people, we are in a position to wisely approach our great task of evangelism. Let there be faithful daily application to the thorough acquisition of these languages ere we assume judgment as to methods and manner of approach. Foundations are being laid and they must be carefully laid in a new land, and utmost deference must be given to the voice of experience in this sphere.
>
> Should God spare me to come again to this field, I look forward to meeting men and women with the closest linguistic contact with, and knowledge of, these people, which are the prerequisites to successful evangelism and true church building.

Mr. Rhoad's first task was to find a site for a mission headquarters in the capital. He was also seeking a bookshop to which a printing press could eventually be added. He found officialdom unwilling to agree to anything in the absence of Dr. Lambie. But in July came the opportunity to extend the SIM's work southward into Gofa province. The previous year, while Rhoad was still in Wallamo, the governor of Gofa province had visited the missionaries at Soddu and had been much impressed by their school. He gave them fifty dollars for it, remarking that he would

like to have a similar school in Gofa. Then he continued his trip
to the capital where he died.

But his son, Dejazmatch Beyenne Merid, who had married
Li'ilt Romanewerq, the Emperor's daughter, was appointed governor in his father's place. He now came to George Rhoad to re-
peat his father's request. Rhoad was very willing to accept the in-
vitation, but he had to make it clear to the governor that this
must depend on the availability of staff. There was the site at
Jimma, too, waiting for someone to move in. Toward the end of
the year it began to appear that it might soon be possible to take
up both openings. Miss Scholl and Mr. Ohman were to be married early in the new year when Miss Scholl had completed her
year in the country. On September 5th Mr. and Mrs. Piepgrass arrived and it was decided that they should go with Miss Irma
Schneck, who had traveled with them, and Miss Sealey who had
come earlier, to Jimma. In the meantime the new missionaries
could study language in the capital in agreement with the general
director's emphasis on learning the language.

The year drew to a close with a flurry of change. On November 2 there was the magnificent scene in St. George's Cathedral
when the Emperor was crowned, a ceremony attended by the
American members of the SIM. The Rasmussens were due to return to Denmark and it was decided that they should be replaced
by the Kirks from Marako. Charles Barton was to marry Miss
Downey on November 20 and she would return with her husband
to Marako. On the same day Reg Annan was planning to marry
Miss Orme and then the couple would return to Lambuda. On
December 15 two new arrivals reached Addis Ababa: Miss
Bessie Martin and Miss Tina McLennan, who was engaged to Mr.
Roke, from New Zealand. The day before Christmas Alfred Roke
arrived in Addis Ababa to greet his fiancée. With him were Miss
Bergsten and Miss Bray from Soddu who had come because Miss
Bergsten was in urgent need of dental care. The two ladies set
up their tent in the garden of the Rhoad's house and awaited
Christmas day, 1930.

4

Spreading Out
1931

In Sidamo province there was a convert whose name was
Hoshe. In February 1931 Hoshe died.

Mr. Cain and Mr. Horn had settled into a regular routine,
spending long hours in intensive language study and cementing
their friendship with their neighbors around Homatcho. The two
men were tired and ready for a break so George Rhoad wrote to
them suggesting that they travel across to Lambuda to be with
the missionaries there for a change. They took Ato Hoshe with
them. Eric Horn was more than tired, he was ill. The men traveled from Lambuda to Marako, intending to go on from there to
Addis Ababa. Clarence Duff agreed to go back with Mr. Cain
to the station at Sidamo because he had been there earlier.

During his short stay at Lambuda, Ato Hoshe ran a nail into
his foot. It caused him some discomfort but he made no complaint then. He set off with the rest of the caravan, leaving the
two missionaries to follow the next day. But word came back to
them that Hoshe was ill:

> The next morning Glen and I went out to Shashogo, and
> found Hoshe, the Sidamo carrier, very ill. His jaws were locked
> and his whole body rigid, and he was in awful pain. There
> wasn't much we knew to do for him, though Glen managed to
> get a little medicine through his teeth after prying them open
> with a spoon. In the afternoon he passed away. He said he was
> not afraid, but was ready to die.[1]

1. Mr. Duff's account of the death of Hoshe, dated February 9, 1931.

The missionaries considered carrying the body back to Sidamo, but the other carriers dissuaded them. So land was purchased right there and a grave dug. His body was wrapped in an Amhara robe and Ato Sabiro, one of the first Christians from Kambatta, helped Duff as he preached briefly in the Gudeila tongue to the twenty or so who stood around. As Mrs. Horn expressed it in a letter written at that time, he was "A Sidamo believer, buried in Gudeila country, wrapped in an Amhara robe, with a brief funeral service conducted by an Australian and an American."

The two missionaries traveled back to Sidamo deep in thought. Glen Cain knew that a witch doctor had warned Hoshe that if he did not leave this new teaching of the missionaries he would die. Now Hoshe was dead. Remarkably there was no bitterness over the death. The other carriers gave a detailed account of the attention paid to Hoshe by the missionaries and the details of the burial which is a vital part of Sidamo culture. To be left unburied, except for the warrior killed in battle, is the crowning dishonor. But Hoshe had been buried with proper respect and they could only attribute his death to God's will.

Clarence Duff adds a fitting postscript to the incident:

> As for Shashogo, I like to think that in planting that first Christian grave there, God has staked out a claim to that country, and will never give it up till its people become his own. "Except a corn of wheat fall into the ground and die, it abideth alone; but if it die, it beareth much fruit."[2] [Jn 12:24]

The first death among the believers in the south of Ethiopia had cast its shadow and now the mission itself faced its first such loss. A son, David Garland, was born to Mrs. Lewis down in Soddu, on February 27, but on March 1 the baby died. The funeral was attended by a great crowd of Wallamo people, among them the governor who comforted Mrs. Lewis with David's words following the death of Bathsheba's child: "I shall go to him, but he will not return to me." [2 Sa 12:23]

In Addis Ababa Mr. Rhoad was planning an ambitious tour of the south, first to Jimma to open the work there, then south to Gofa to open that station, then north to Soddu for a mission con-

2. Ibid. His words were prophetic for in 1958 I spent a night in one of the Shashogo churches which today form part of the great complex of the Kambatta church fellowship.

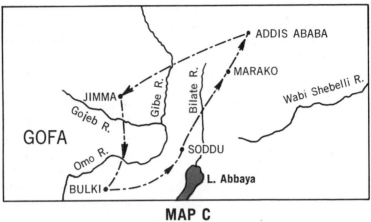

MAP C
GEORGE RHOAD'S TRIP

ference and then, by way of Marako, back to Addis Ababa. On February 18 Walter Ohman was married to Marcella Scholl, the first American couple ever married in Ethiopia. They were to spend their honeymoon trekking down to Soddu and then south to Gofa where they would meet Mr. Rhoad. See map C.

Their caravan went ahead of them on the afternoon of the wedding, and camp was set up ready for their arrival, at Fure, just on the outskirts of the city and at that time the end of the motor road to the south. George Rhoad drove the young couple out in his car: the only touch of luxury they were to experience in the two and a half months that would elapse before they reached Bulki, in Gofa province. Three hundred miles lay between them and their destination.

Their first breakfast together was eaten before sunrise by the light of their campfire. Their daily routine soon fixed itself into a pattern: six to eight hours of riding, lunch and then their carriers were sent off to any village in the area telling the people that medical care from Mrs. Ohman, a registered nurse, was available. Each evening Walter Ohman would preach to any who came to listen to his Bible stories.

On the fourth night they reached Marako; four more days brought them to Lambuda, and then came the long stage to Wallamo. There they paused for a couple of weeks, waiting for Mr. Rhoad's order to move into Gofa.

George Rhoad's party had left Addis Ababa, heading for Jimma in March. With him went Mr. and Mrs. Piepgrass, Miss Schneck and Miss Sealey, all to remain at Jimma. Miss Ferron had been appointed mission treasurer and so her place as secretary to the director was taken by Miss Martin. With the missionaries settled in at Qochi, in Jimma, the Rhoads and Miss Martin turned southward to cross over both Gojeb and Omo gorges to reach Bulki where the Ohmans and Laurie Davison, appointed to help them at the new station, were to be awaiting them.

The Ohmans' trip from Soddu to Bulki had proved interesting. On April 16, along with Mr. Davison, they had left Soddu. As usual they had sent their caravan on ahead to set up camp for them. But that evening they were quite unable to locate the camp. Fortunately, one of the Wallamos in their party had a friend who lived nearby. His second wife had recently deserted him. Since Wallamo custom requires a separate hut for each wife, her hut was vacant. The three missionaries, their Ethiopian companions and their mules spent the night there. Supper was something of a problem, for all their supplies were with their pack mules. But as they left Soddu, Mrs. Lewis had given them a package which, on inspection, proved to contain chicken loaf and chocolate cake. So they cheerfully dined on that. With equal enthusiasm they broke their fast the next morning on the same fare.

The following morning their caravan caught up with them, the porters having taken the opportunity of a final spree in Soddu. They had camped for the night a mile or two behind the missionaries. So the party headed south again and at last reached Gofa province. Here the plains ended and great mountain ranges reared up ahead of them. Their path began to be crossed by rushing streams, and finally they reached the Maze river which was at flood level. The supply boxes were swathed in the canvas of the tents and floated across by the muleteers. Then the mules were driven into the water and allowed to swim across with the muleteers hanging onto their tails. From that point on the little party received gifts of sheep, goats, eggs, or a bullock each evening from the local governors.

After fourteen days of travel they reached Hotto, some thirty minutes ride from Bulki. There the governor, Dejazmatch Beyenne, had assigned them a camping site. They pitched their tents and the next day the governor and his chief men, all dressed in their ceremonial lion's mane headdresses, received the missionaries at Bulki. While in the company of these others, the governor would use only Amharic which was not understood by the missionaries who had learned Wallamo, but the following day he showed that he also spoke perfect Wallamo.

In the first few days the missionaries began surveying the area and were a little discouraged by the seemingly sparse population, sparse certainly when compared with Wallamo. But when Mr. Rhoad arrived ten days later, he assured them that there were some forty to fifty thousand people living in the area centered on Bulki, and he encouraged them to press on with their plans. These included the school, requested by the governor. Mrs. Ohman already had a medical work under way.

Assured that the three missionaries were settled into the new work, Mr. and Mrs. Rhoad with Miss Martin headed for Wallamo where a conference had been arranged for the missionaries from Wallamo, Kambatta and Sidamo to discuss some of the problems inseparable from a growing work. On June 3 the conference began with the Lewises, Miss Bray and Miss Jean Cable, who was to move to Bulki after the rains, everyone from Soddu, Mr. Roke and Mr. Cain from Homatcho, and Clarence Duff from Lambuda.

The financing of schools was discussed and the principle by which school fees were linked to earning power was approved. A minimum fee of one *timun*,[3] or twenty-five cents, per month was agreed upon. The missionaries involved with the schools had their problems:

> Mr. Rhoad emphasized the importance of coming to an agreement on the stations as to how many are to be engaged in school activities, and how far these activities are to involve them. He advised that only those really necessary be engaged in this work. The one in charge, however, should always have opportunity to go out into the villages. For this reason others on

3. The Ethiopian monetary system is confusing to the beginner. Four francs make ten cents, twenty-five cents make a *simuni,* formerly a *timun,* fifty cents make a shilling, one hundred cents make a dollar and ten dollars make a pound. The Marie Therese dollar is no longer legal tender, but in 1958 it was worth approximately two dollars and thirty cents. The five cent piece is often called a *bekenna,* but in some areas is called one cent, while in Kambatta the ten cent piece is referred to as one cent. In 1973 one U.S. dollar was worth just over two Ethiopian dollars.

the station should expect to co-operate by substituting or assisting, when necessary.[4]

The missionaries had also come up against the problem of the Ethiopic script. This script was used for writing Ge'ez, but was later modified to meet the needs of the Amharic language, which differs from Ge'ez in a number of ways: the laryngals have disappeared and a number of palatalized consonants have appeared. Mr. Rhoad explained that mission policy must follow government policy of retaining the syllabary. They would then make such adaptations as might be necessary for use with languages such as Galla. Obviously the use of Roman script in teaching the people would have left them unable to read the proclamations of their own government. Whether the decision to retain the Ethiopic script, a decision which had but recently been taken by the government, was the correct one or not is, of course, another matter.

After the conference the Rhoad party accompanied Duff to Kambatta. Earlier in the year Rhoad had suggested to Duff that a thorough survey of the Kambatta district should be made and Duff soon realized that he had to deal with two related groups, the Hadya or Gudeila around Hosanna, and the Kambatta to the southeast. To reach the Kambatta people Duff had prospected the area near Ambaricho mountain close by the Bezanna stream and now Duff was anxious to get the director's approval of the location so that negotiations on a contract could begin. Rhoad looked the site over and gave his approval: this could be the SIM's second location in Kambatta. So Mr. Rhoad moved on to Marako, where he found Eric Horn who accompanied him to Addis Ababa. After a fortnight in the capital, Mr. Horn felt well enough to return to his work in Sidamo.

The rainy season in Gofa had set in. To try to keep the streaming torrents out of their tents, the men dug trenches outside, and banked straw around the trailing canvas. Contemptuously the rain filled the trenches and swirled away the straw. They abandoned the tents and moved into two Gofa huts, one at each end of their piece of land. Both leaked abominably and were abysmally dark. Walter Ohman tried to correct this by cutting window spaces in the walls, but he soon found that the rain which beat in these impromptu openings was a greater inconvenience than the gloom,

4. "Soddu Conference Minutes," p. 2.

so he boarded them over again. They lived in daily expectation of the arrival of the rest of their supplies, but word reached them from Soddu that they could expect nothing until after the rains.

At nighttime the three missionaries would gather in one of the two huts, by the light of a pressure lantern, and, with blankets wrapped around them, try to study. But with the end of the rains came Jean Cable from Soddu. On August 1 she left Soddu, accompanied by the Lewises as far as the Demi river. Then she traveled three more days until she reached the Maze river where she found Walter Ohman waiting to escort her into Bulki. Now the building work could go ahead once more: three two-roomed huts were planned, one for the Ohmans, one for Mr. Davison and one for Miss Cable.

One side of their rainy season existence had puzzled the missionaries at Bulki: in spite of the continual rain they had regularly been supplied with a bundle of dry wood for the fires. Without fail it would be found outside their hut each morning. Curious to discover where this came from, they finally located their benefactor in a valley some two thousand feet below them. The man was a slave, but he took it upon himself to ensure that the strangers on the mountain above should have dry wood to kindle their fires each day.

At this time slavery was still common in the south. At the inter-mission prayer meeting held in Addis Ababa on April of that year Miss Ferron reported:

> We might mention the matter of slave-raiding in Wallamo country. Perhaps you are not troubled with this in the parts of Abyssinia where you are working. The Governor of Wallamo is doing all he can to put a stop to it, for which we are thankful. Not so very long ago, only about a quarter of a mile from the station, a woman and two men were killed and two children taken away by slave raiders, although the children were later recovered.[5]

Dufarsha, an escaped slave, was one of the first Gofa converts. Since the Gofa language is merely a dialect of the Wallamo language which Mr. Ohman had learned, he had little trouble in making himself understood. He began to translate Mark's gospel into

5. Report of inter-mission prayer meeting held in Addis Ababa on Thursday, April 16, 1931, by Miss Ferron.

the Gofa dialect. One day as he was working on his translation, seated as usual outside the house, he asked his wife if she would care to hear the story of the prodigal son in the Gofa language. As he read it aloud a young Shankalla[6] who was cutting grass nearby, listened, smiling his approval from time to time. When he had finished Mr. Ohman asked the young man, Dufarsha, if he liked the story. He said that he did and that he had heard the same story before. The evening before he had been caring for one of the Wallamos, who had come with the Ohmans from Soddu and was sick. The Wallamo had told him the same story. Dufarsha believed what he heard about God and he decided to become a Christian. He told the Ohmans his story.

When he was a boy he was caring for cattle when two men carried him off as a slave. Again and again he tried to escape. At last, when he was about sixteen years old he managed to reach the very borders of his own country. There he took refuge with a woman whom both he and his parents had known. She was a "prophetess," and told him that he would one day reach his own people, and then he would hear "some good news and some bad news." The next morning Dufarsha was recaptured and carried back into slavery. Two more years passed and again he fled. At last he reached his home. His relatives began to tell him the news: both his mother and father had died and their cattle were either dead or stolen. And then he asked them, "Now you have told me all bad news. What is the good news?" His relatives were perplexed. They knew only bad news. From that time until he met the missionaries Dufarsha had been seeking the good news that had been promised him.

Nearly forty years later Walter Ohman revisited Bulki. He found Dufarsha: the church built on his land was the first church to be built amongst the Shankalla people. Walter Ohman said simply, "All my forty years on the field were worth this testimony. If Dufarsha only were saved it was well worth while."[7]

At the end of 1931 the school at Bulki was open. There were Sunday services and a Wednesday evening gathering. Regularly

6. This is the name used in Ethiopia to describe several tribes mainly inhabiting the southern and western borderlands. Their principal characteristic is the pronounced negroid features common to them all. The name may be used as an insult.
7. From the tape prepared by Rev. and Mrs. Ohman.

the missionaries visited their neighbors. Their genuine affection for the Gofa people was returned. When Mr. Ohman began to build a home for himself and his wife, he was astonished to find all the neighbors presenting themselves at the building site. They explained that it was the custom of the Gofa people that if a man were building a house, all of his neighbors should assist him without expecting any pay, so they were all contributing a day's work.

In Wallamo Miss Bergsten was back again, having traveled from Addis Ababa with Princess Romanewerq. The missionaries in Sidamo were planning to extend the work and on November 20 Mr. Cain and Mr. Roke made a trip into Darassa country, south of Homatcho, prospecting for a new station. The year had also brought new blood into the mission. Mr. and Mrs. Couser arrived in May, together with Cliff Mitchell. In November Miss Winifred Robertson, who had been presented at court in London, arrived with Miss Myrtle Jenkins and Miss M. A. McMillan, known to everyone as Daisy. The Rasmussens had resigned from the mission after their return to Denmark but even so the personnel now totaled thirty-five.

Illness was beginning to hit the mission, however. Both Mr. and Mrs. Kirk underwent operations for appendicitis. Mrs. Couser was operated on for an extra-uterine pregnancy and was seriously ill. Mrs. Lewis was having goiter trouble. Mr. Ohman appeared to have strained his heart. But on the other side of the ledger could be seen the first results of their labors: in all three of the pioneer areas the first Christians of the great church which was yet to come stood firm.

5

Commitment
1932

On January 7 of the new year Mrs. Couser died. The next day her body was laid to rest in the Gulele cemetery. There were many health problems that year. Glen Cain had to be flown out from Homatcho in the emperor's plane, Earl Lewis had an operation, and in Soddu Walter Ohman had his appendix removed. Selma Bergsten's health was failing again. In the capital the Kirk family was shaken up when their truck overturned. Mrs. Kirk and Paul were in shock, and Mr. Kirk had several ribs fractured.

Mr. Rhoad was still attempting to finalize an agreement for two sites he had picked out in Addis Ababa. One, for a headquarters, was situated some three miles out of the city center on a hill overlooking the Akaki River, not far from where the Princess Tsehai Memorial Hospital now stands. The second, two miles further west, at Fure, had over a hundred acres of land and was very suitable for a leprosarium. But without Lambie nothing could be finalized.[1] He came back in February, and within a few weeks the negotiations for these two sites were completed.

Five new missionaries accompanied the Lambies: Dr. Hooper, who was to go to Soddu to commence medical work until the leprosarium in Addis Ababa was ready for him and Don Davies would remain temporarily in the capital to help with building the headquarters but would eventually go to Jimma. His fiancée, Ruth Sykes, would stay in Addis Ababa for language study with Leona MacGregor whose eventual destination was Soddu where

1. In the years before the Italian occupation the mission was known in Ethiopia simply as "Dr. Lambie's mission."

she would help with the medical work. Marion Walker became
the director's secretary. Although the year was a bad one for
health, it was an outstandingly good one for new workers. John
Phillips went to Kambatta after a spell on the Addis Ababa building work. Rev. James Luckman went to Bulki after assisting Cliff
Mitchell in building the Yirga Alem station for a short time. Dr.
Hooper's daughter, Helen, who had been working in India, remained in Addis Ababa. Nick Simponis, a self-styled Los Angeles
soda jerk, spent his first year working among his fellow-Greeks
(he was a naturalized American) before going to Soddu. And
there was Zillah Walsh who was to undergo weeks of wandering
in Kambatta following the Italian invasion. Two days after Christmas, a party of nine missionaries and three children arrived from
America.

Building work got under way in Addis Ababa. Mrs. Lambie
had been in close touch with the American Mission to Lepers and
they had agreed to make available five thousand dollars a year for
five years so that a leprosarium could be built in Ethiopia. Other
money came in for the project which moved ahead rapidly. In
April, Eric Horn left Homatcho for a bookshop work in Addis
Ababa and spent the next months negotiating for property and
organizing supplies. Not all of the missionaries were happy about
the large-scale building operations in the capital, nor was there
complete agreement over the transfer of the mission headquarters
from the south to the capital. The feeling of some was that the
initial impetus of the mission's drive south was being lost and the
mission was being swamped by institutional work.

But there was the positive side, too. Through the south the first
converts were being gathered in. The question of baptism had
arisen. Who should examine the converts to decide their fitness
for baptism? Mr. Cain, Mr. Duff and Mr. Lewis wrote to the field
directors, Rhoad and Lambie, asking for clarification of mission
policy. A conference was called at Soddu for May 16-18.

The minutes of the conference are restrained but it is clear that
some of the missionaries could not see the value of having the
directors coming to their stations to examine candidates for baptism. The fairly rigid approach advocated by Mr. Rhoad con-
trasted with the more relaxed attitude of the younger men:

There was considerable discussion as to the necessity of prescribed procedure being laid down for the mission as a whole, or as to whether it might not better be left to the Field Directors and the missionaries, as guided by the Spirit, as the question had to be faced in separate fields.

The discussion continued but it seemed impossible to reach a decision. Since the matter of baptism was pressing in Sidamo, Dr. Lambie invited Glen Cain to give a report on the work there. He told of "the calling of the first believers, their choosing of elders, their clear-cut testimonies, their spiritual discernment and judgment" and he said that "a most interesting phase of the work there had been the springing up of a group of believers at some distance from the station, as a result of the testimonies of native Christians."

In a rather odd summary the minutes record:

> The general conviction, as expressed by Mr. Rhoad, Dr. Lambie and others was, that from the evidences submitted there were apparently believers in Sidamo ready for baptism.

The discussion on baptism continued all morning the next day. In the afternoon the discussion terminated abruptly when "Mr. Rhoad expressed himself of the persuasion that it would be better to leave the whole matter of baptism to be decided under the provisions of our constitution," which was precisely what the younger missionaries objected to.

The subject was temporarily dropped. The question of the observation of Christmas and Easter arose: should the Western calendar be followed or the calendar of the Orthodox church? It was agreed to observe the latter; however, the days were to be regarded as opportunities for preaching rather than holidays.

The issue of the Addis Ababa building program came next. Mr. Rhoad explained the history of the decision to move headquarters from Soddu to Addis Ababa and emphasized the need for a forwarding base in the capital which could also function as a training home for new missionaries and a center for evangelization in Addis Ababa. This third point represents a break with earlier strategy, for Dr. Lambie had stated in his report to the board members of the AFM that while a forwarding base in Addis Ababa was needed, no definite mission work was to be undertaken there, "as the Swedish and American Missions both have stations here, as well as the Adventists," and in 1930, when the move to Addis Ababa had been proposed by Dr. Bingham, the statement was made that "it is not intended in any way to overlap the work of the other missions located there."

A letter was read from Eric Horn confirming that, in his opinion, the Addis Ababa program was intended "definitely to facilitate the evangelization of the south." The next day Dr. Lambie gave a brief account of the projected leprosarium which appeared to satisfy the conference.

Mr. Rhoad was due to leave for furlough in June, and Dr. Lambie proposed that a letter of appreciation to Mrs. Rhoad for her work in language teaching might be written and this was agreed to. Then Lambie announced that Dr. Bingham had asked Mr. Rhoad to act as deputy general director of the SIM during his own absence on a sabbatical year.

On the final day of the conference Dr. Lambie announced the appointment of the first district superintendents:

Western district (Jimma)	Mr. Piepgrass
Eastern district (Sidamo)	Mr. Cain
Southern district (Wallamo and Gofa)	Mr. Ohman
Northern district (Kambatta and Gurage)	Mr. Duff

Then the principal subject of the conference was again considered: baptismal procedure. The conference accepted Dr. Lambie's resolution:

> We adhere to the simplicity of the "Principles and Practice," and we recommend that all cases of prospective candidates for baptism be most prayerfully and carefully considered by the missionaries at the station, with the Field Directors and those whom they may wish to associate with them.

Those present at this very important conference were Dr. Lambie and Rev. George Rhoad from Addis Ababa, Mr. Barton from Marako, Mr. and Mrs. Lewis, Dr. Hooper, Miss Bray and Miss Bergsten from Wallamo, Mr. Cain from Sidamo, Mr. and Mrs. Annan, Mr. Duff and Mr. Couser from Kambatta and Mr. and Mrs. Ohman from Gofa.

On June 19, Mr. Rhoad and his wife left for furlough and to take up his post as deputy general director. In February 1934 he cabled his resignation from the SIM to Dr. Bingham who at that time was visiting Ethiopia. Mr. Rhoad's years with the mission had not been easy ones. He had traveled hundreds of miles by mule, had often been misunderstood and had the great disadvantage of being inevitably compared with Dr. Lambie. Rev. Eric Horn wrote:

> While it is true that Dr. Lambie had had prior experience of dealing with Ethiopian officials, and that there were often disagreements between the two leaders, the Mission owes a tremendous debt to Mr. Rhoad in the administrative sphere, as well as for the considerable financial resources which he used in the interests of the work. While there was, on the part of we young and inexperienced missionaries, a certain amount of criticism of our two leaders at various times, we owe much to them.

After the conference Dr. Lambie wrote briefly to Dr. Bingham about it but left Dr. Hooper, who had been a member of the SIM home council, to fill in details. That the conference was critical of the SIM leadership in Ethiopia is suggested by Lambie's words:

> I think Dr. Hooper is going to write to you more fully about it and certainly I shall be glad if he does so, as coming from him, as a member of the Home Council, I feel it is perhaps more appropriate than either from George or myself.[2]

In the same letter Dr. Lambie passes on an account of the beginning of a church in Sidamo. A Sidamo convert moved his home ten or fifteen miles away and began to preach to his new neighbors. At first it was very discouraging: no one would listen and when he prayed, the people simply walked off and left him or else heaped insults on him. He went to Cain for advice and was told to persevere. A few months later he was back to say that he had one convert; a little later there were three and after a month or so there were eight and they wanted to build a church.

Mr. Cain wrote an account of those early days:

> Sunday's meeting was four full hours and such a time of heart searching I have never seen. One fellow confessed to having stolen some *inset* [*Ensete Ventrioscum*][3] from one of the elders, with a promise to pay all back in full. Some five or six

2. Letter from Lambie to Bingham, June 1, 1932.
3. *Ensete Ventrioscum* closely resembles the banana tree but gives no fruit. The lower part of the stem yields a starchy fiber which is used to produce a rather coarse flour.

confessed to thefts of money, promising to pay all back to respective owners. Five confessed adultery.

After this they called upon me to tell them what was the next thing to do according to the Bible. I explained that the Word says if we confessed He was faithful and just to forgive. At this point a suggestion was thrown out by a young Amhara that all should declare their determination for the future, whether they intended to go on with all their hearts and fully obey the teaching of Christ or not. Another fellow replied: "But the Word says that no one must take more wives, at least add wives, and this a Sidamo can't promise to keep."

Wednesday afternoon the meeting continued. Feeling again ran high, for a man who failed to carry on his family line is cursed of his fellow-men, according to Sidamo thinking, and surely under the curse of God. According to Sidamo law, if a man takes a wife and she is barren, he is bound to take others until he has male heirs. The Bible calls this adultery and here came the cause of the struggle. By the talk it looked as though about four or five only would stand by the Word. Indeed it was a tense moment. The elders said, "What shall we do?" I said, "Let me show you a short way. If some are going to reject Christ's words, they reject Him as master, and on account of this there will be division." I called upon the oldest elder to declare himself and very beautifully and clearly he did, saying that he had believed the Word and had been saved and would now continue in obedience to that Word. The second elder said, "My position is that also." The third said, "I have enough trouble with one wife; the Word for me!" The fourth, Ortisa by name, said, "I have no heir and can't very well if I obey the Word; if God gives me an heir or no heir I will not go back, I will obey the words of Jesus Christ."

After this they addressed me again: "Leave it with us now, we shall do the rest." The first man they asked, a convert of a month ago, stumbled and said he could not answer, but that he wanted to talk with the others who had not decided, and so about fifteen of them went out to talk. One by one they came back and said, "We determine to obey the Word," until the last two came and said "We cannot." One was a polygamist with two wives, who said that both wives had many children and if one was to go away he would simply have to take another in her place to care for the children. The other was a single fellow who said he was too poor to buy a wife and would only be

able to get a wife by taking a runaway wife, which, of course,
is adultery.

Eventually the church ruled that marriages could only be arranged by believers after approval by the elders. A young man
named Kowada, however, arranged a marriage to a woman of
whom the elders could not approve. A three-day conference of all
believers was called, at which all were invited to confess their
faults. In the first round of confessions the matter of eating meat
from animals sacrificed to the spirits was raised. The missionaries
referred the elders to Paul's first letter to the church at Corinth
which deals with the subject. It was after this matter had been
settled that Kowada admitted his marriage plans.

The elders discussed the situation and found that the arrangements could, without difficulty, be cancelled. Kowada could be
fined. But one elder was concerned that over the months sins were
being confessed and forgiven and shortly afterward the same
sins were repeated by the same people. Sin was not taken seriously. Again the missionaries were asked for advice. Only a few days
previously they had learned the word used in the Sidamo language
for expulsion from the tribe. As soon as the missionaries introduced this word the elders took it up. They recognized the seriousness of expulsion from the church, but they needed some sanction
to bring home to the believers the seriousness of repeated failure.
Kowada's case was considered for a further three days. In the end
it was decided not to invoke this extreme penalty in his case. But
on later occasions it was used and resulted in a very evident stif-
fening of moral standards.

Medical work had opened the way into the homes of the Sidamo people. The first visits to a home came when a woman with
an eye infection had to be treated over a period of months. A
young man named Namasha was added to the church when he
came in for treatment of a bullet wound in the leg, received from
a slave-raiding party. As the number of converts grew, the question
of baptism became pressing. Initially it appeared possible that as
many as twenty might be eligible, but the process of examination
reduced the number steadily. And some withdrew from this clear
break with the society they knew. Candidates were examined by
their fellow believers.

The first candidate to be examined was told that he must wait:

he had recently sent away his wife and the reason for this was not clear. The second candidate had two wives. The church had sent two men to his village and they learned that he had pulled down the fences around the demon shrines and used the wood for cooking. He did not share in the spirit sacrifices. He himself made it clear that he understood the implications of the new faith. They decided that he should be baptized, but he was told that he must not take more wives, nor replace one if in some way she was separated from him. And further he could not be considered for election as a church elder.

The third man had been under a witch doctor's curse prohibiting him from eating goat meat. When he ate it he was invariably taken ill. After becoming a Christian, however, his brother, already a believer, brought him some of the forbidden meat to test the genuineness of his faith. He ate the meat and suffered no ill effects. The story was accepted as evidence of genuine conversion and the man was approved for baptism. This same man's mother was another candidate. In view of her age she was excused from the usual requirement that she learn to read and the usual lengthy catechism class. Her simple words expressed a genuine faith, and she was included in the party for baptism.

Following her was a younger woman whose husband was already a believer, She was quickly approved, and so they came to the last candidate, a man named Kanune. He had been requesting baptism for a long time. At Soddu Dr. Hooper had removed his appendix. He had worked hard to repay the debts which accumulated during his illness. But when the elders questioned him it was clear that, in addition to the failings he was willing to confess, there was at least one moral lapse that he was hoping to pass over. A remark from one of the elders, however, showed him that his lapse was known:

> This remark prompted a sad confession from Kanune of a grievous moral offence which he was evidently intending to leave unconfessed. "Ahum", said the elder, "And you did that since you professed to believe, did you?" Kanune replied that he had.
>
> "And do you mean to say that you committed that sin in the full expectation of baptism, thinking that you could hide it

on this day, or simply confess it and be received into our fellowship?"

Kanune fell right into the trap that had been set for him and said "Yes."

The consequence of this little interchange was that Kanune's case had to be discussed at great length, and proved to be the one case in which the advice of the missionaries was sought. Up to this point they had sat in silence. Some of the elders felt that since he had confessed, the man should be accepted, while others mistrusted the tardiness in his confession. It was agreed to ask the missionaries. They suggested that, as in the case of the first candidate, he should be asked to wait. The elders agreed and when Kanune failed to present himself for the next baptism, the elders felt that time had justified their course of action.

Confession played a prominent part in church life, especially before a communion service. On one occasion a church member confessed that he held a grudge against the missionaries since they had underpaid him for some work he had done for them. According to custom a spokesman was appointed for the man and he then asked the missionaries for an explanation. The affair proved to be a misunderstanding: in paying the man the missionaries had given him a little extra as a mark of appreciation for quality work and the extra had upset his calculations. He thought that he had received less than expected. This is understandable where barter is more common than the use of money. The matter was explained to the workman who at once accepted the explanation and apologized for harboring a grievance.

Everything was ready in Sidamo for the first baptismal service, but in the capital Dr. Lambie had too many commitments to enable him to visit Homatcho just then. In September Dr. J. Oswald Smith of the People's Church in Toronto came on a brief visit. A number of SIM missionaries have received their support from Dr. Smith's church and so Lambie was anxious to show him something of the work in Ethiopia. Together with Miss Robertson, who had been appointed to the new work planned for Yirga Alem, Dr. Lambie and Dr. Smith set off for a brief tour of the stations in the south. But before reaching even Marako, the first station, Dr. Smith was forced to turn back because he was

ill and Lambie rode back to the capital with him, leaving Miss
Robertson to press on to Marako alone.

By this time the mission work was expanding on every hand.
Duff, with the help of his two advisers, Ato Shibashi and Ato
Muluneh, was able to finalize an agreement with Ato Yambo for
a piece of land at Durami among the Kambatta people. In Sidamo, Dejazmatch Biru had been promoted to war minister and replaced as governor-general of Sidamo province by Ras Desta, son-
in-law of the Emperor. He had pushed ahead with plans to move
the capital to Yirga Alem[4] and Lambie was anxious to open a
work there. Up in the mountains of Gofa, Ras Desta's brother,
Dejazmatch Ababa, was governor and he invited the mission to
open a station at Chencha, his capital.

In the area south of Sidamo, Glen Cain and Alfred Roke had
located a suitable site for a mission station among the Darassa
people, some thirty miles south of Homatcho, at Tutitti. In the
capital the building work was going ahead. On November 15 the
Emperor and many of the Ethiopian nobility were present at the
laying of the cornerstone of the new leprosarium. Three days later
Eric Horn opened the new SIM bookshop in Addis Ababa. It was
clearly time to redeploy the missionaries and to open the new
mission stations.

Cliff Mitchell and Miss Jenkins were married in November and
appointed to Tutitti. In December Dr. Lambie left the capital on
yet another round tour, first to Sidamo to attend the baptismal
service, then to negotiate a mission site at Yirga Alem and to
send the Mitchells on to Tutitti. The next call would be at Soddu,
where he would leave Miss MacGregor, to replace Miss Bergsten
and Miss Bray, who could then go on to Chencha. Then he traveled back to Lambuda to check on the site at Durami, and so
back to Addis Ababa again.

On December 25, 1932, Dr. Lambie and Mr. Cain baptized four
men by immersion. On the day before Christmas Cain and Duff,
together with Cliff Mitchell, hopefully on his way to Tutitti, and
Dr. Hooper, who rode across from Soddu to witness the event,
dammed up the small stream which flowed at the bottom of the
hill near the mission station at Homatcho, and turned a small area

4. Unfortunately he changed the site from that recommended by Dr.
Lambie, moving it to a lower location which subsequently proved malarial.

into a lake. To the last, things were difficult for the candidates. Dr. Hooper wrote:

> The first one to enter the water was, that morning, confronted by his whole family. His wife clung to him to prevent him and said she would leave him if he were immersed. His mother cried and plead, and threatened to disown and disinherit her son if he should disobey her command. He was determined to follow the Lord. The brother and others of family and friends barred the door of the hut and had refused to let him go.

Neither Marion Walker, Dr. Lambie's secretary, nor Mrs. Lambie actually witnessed the baptism although both were at Homatcho. Inexplicably the men failed to call them to witness the historic event. Afterward Marion Walker wrote to Syvilla Horn:[5]

> They were afraid Dr. and Mr. C. were going to do all sorts of things and the wife and mother set up an awful howl when the one elder went into the water. They thought he was being drowned for sure!

Dr. Lambie went to see Ras Desta about a mission location at Yirga Alem and was met with a counterproposal: they might have the site if the mission would loan Mr. Mitchell to assist in the initial laying out of the new capital. So the Mitchells moved into Yirga Alem: over 1,400 houses were built in the first year at Yirga Alem, a measure of the Mitchells' anxiety to get on to Tutitti.

Another year had drawn to a close. There were now fifty-five SIM missionaries in the country. Lambie headed over to Wallamo to see about a new advance there.

5. Miss Ferron and Mr. Horn were married on June 2.

6

Some Fundamentals
1933

At Soddu it was agreed that Miss MacGregor would remain to replace Miss Bray in the medical work, while Miss Bray and Miss Bergsten opened up the new work in Gamo province at Chencha. The Kirks could then be spared from the building work in Addis Ababa; Dr. Lambie would send them south on his return to the capital.

In Kambatta, Duff was anxious to occupy the new mission site at Durami, and he had the staff to do it. Nine missionaries reached Addis Ababa two days after Christmas: Dr. Roberts, who was to release Dr. Hooper from Soddu to take up the leprosarium work in Addis Ababa, and his wife; Mr. and Mrs. Street who would eventually go to Chencha; Mr. John Trewin, who went with them; Mary Berger, a nurse; Margaret Miller; Frances Ottinger and Nell Sharretts, who resigned from the mission the following year. Duff went up to Addis Ababa to escort Dr. and Mrs. Roberts on their way to Soddu, to get Mr. Luckman on his way to assist in the building work at Yirga Alem and to bring John Phillips to Kambatta for the new station at Durami if Lambie approved.

In February Dr. Lambie arrived at Lambuda, accompanied by Dr. Hooper on his way to the leprosarium work. The whole party went out to inspect the site at Durami which proved to be satisfactory. On March 18 Duff and John Phillips pitched their tents there. Dr. Lambie continued his long round tour, pausing at Marako to collect Miss Robertson, who was still patiently waiting there after her attempt in September to reach her station at Yirga Alem was frustrated by Dr. Smith's illness. Back in the capital Lambie arranged for the Kirks to leave at once for Chencha and for Miss Robertson to go with them.

This time Miss Robertson was halfway between Marako and Lambuda when illness struck again: this time it was rheumatic fever. She was carried into Lambuda on an improvised stretcher. The Kirks left her there while John Phillips was called in from Durami and sent off to report on the situation to Lambie. The opening of the Durami work had left the Annans alone at Lambuda and they could not cope with the added responsibility of Miss Robertson's illness. Phillips returned with Peggy Miller and Zillah Walsh, a nurse, who were to remain at Lambuda and he also escorted three ladies for the Soddu work.

But 1933 was to prove the year when illness took toll of the mission repeatedly. On May 25, without any warning that she was even ill, Bessie Martin died at Marako, just as evening prayers ended. Freda Horn, younger sister of Eric Horn, was sent down to Marako to be with Miss McMillan. On June 1 Lambie flew down to Kambatta in the Emperor's plane and brought Miss Robertson back to the capital: she had suffered serious heart damage and medical care was imperative. In July Glen Cain was ill with heart trouble and he also had to be flown to Addis Ababa. But this illness had a happy ending to it. As both Cain and Miss Robertson needed medical attention they were, contrary to normal mission practice, allowed to travel back to New Zealand on the same boat. Eric Horn's uncle, then chairman of the SIM's New Zealand council married them in Auckland.

In Sidamo the Mitchells, released from their building work at Yirga Alem, were no sooner settled into Tutitti than Cliff Mitchell contracted typhus. His wife nursed him until she, too, was taken ill with the disease and then Leona MacGregor came over to help them. In Lambuda both Peggy Miller and Zillah Walsh had typhus too. In Addis Ababa Fred Russell of the Presbyterian mission caught it and so did Dr. Wilson's wife. In September Luckman was at Soddu for an appendectomy and little Ruth Lewis had to have an operation for mastoid. Mrs. Kirk was also sick.

Up in the mountains of Gamo Miss Bray and Miss Bergsten settled into a rented house in the town of Chencha. Miss Bray opened a clinic and two or three times a week the two women would ride out to spend a whole day among the people. They would sit at the stream near the Dorze village, famous throughout Ethiopia for its weaving, and try to talk with the women who came down to wash. At least the move did not present any great language difficulty since the Gamo language is a dialect of Wallamo. But when the missionaries came anywhere near the women they would simply run away. Miss Bergsten says candidly, "It all seemed fruitless." At last the Kirks arrived, and a few days later Jean Cable came in from Bulki, to the south. She was on her way to Soddu and furlough; her father was celebrating fifty years in medical practice in Forfar, Angus, Scotland, and the family wanted her there. She had been ill and her furlough was approved. But her arrival at Chencha unsettled Miss Bray. She had been in Ethiopia for four and a half years and was discouraged by the work at Chencha. She was older than most new missionaries and perhaps lacked the resilience which some enjoyed. At all events this contact with Miss Cable turned Ruth Bray's thoughts homeward. She had her passage money. Swiftly she packed and accompanied Miss Bray to Soddu, to Addis Ababa and so on to furlough.

Miss Bergsten writes:

> I stayed on in the large, oblong, Amhara house. It was one huge room where we had our cots, folding table and chairs. [We] made a long permanent table out of some split trees, and on that we kept all our food supplies. There was plenty of room for saddles, grain for the mules, our own wood for the cooking, which we did over an open fire outside. Seemingly countless big rats had their race-course in the room. Still, we were not crowded!

Mrs. Kirk was not well, either. Dr. Roberts made a hurried trip up the mountain to treat her and the little party soldiered on through the rains. But by October it was clear that Mrs. Kirk needed more medical attention. Selma Bergsten could not be left in Chencha alone and so all three made their way to Soddu. There Nick Simponis was waiting for them, having been appointed to Chencha, and he returned up the mountain with Mr. Kirk. They had some opportunity for preaching, once at a great funeral at nearby Ocholo mountain. Then Kirk went back to Soddu and

Simponis was alone until Dr. Lambie arrived. Field council was to be held in Soddu and Lambie decided to head south early to examine the situation at first hand. Lambie's party was met by five half-grown lions, restrained only by ropes held by some young lads, sent out as an escort by the governor. The governor welcomed Lambie and suggested that Beli, out from Chencha toward Ocholo, might be a better spot for the mission than in the town. Lambie promised to send someone in from Soddu to obtain a suitable spot and, leaving Simponis in the house at Chencha, Dr. Lambie, his wife and his secretary, Miss Walker, went off to Soddu and the council meetings.

A few days later Clarence Duff arrived in Chencha and the two men went out to Beli to choose a site for their new mission station. A suitable place was found and Duff was able to finalize a contract with the owner of the land. Remembering what it was like to live in a tent, Duff also purchased a Dorze house for Simponis. These houses are constructed principally from bamboo and so it was no great difficulty to have the house dug up and then transported bodily across the valley to be set up on the mission property. Scores of pairs of legs dangled beneath the huge house as, like some monstrous cross between a snail and a centipede, the hut lurched across the lush green of the hillside. With Simponis comfortably settled, Clarence Duff left him alone again.

Down at Soddu the work was very encouraging. The foundation of the work had been visiting the people. Even while the early building work was in progress Mr. Ohman and Clarence Duff had taken time each day to visit the homes of the people living near Otona. They soon picked up the phrase "What is this?" in the Wallamo language and they used it tirelessly, adding steadily to their vocabulary. The succeeding missionaries had followed the example set by the pioneers. Miss Bergsten and Mrs. Lewis spent hours each day in the homes of the women.

Mrs. Lewis organized a daily class for the children and Miss Bergsten began another for mission employees and any others who wanted to attend. Mr. Lewis arranged his visiting in the evening, when he could be reasonably sure of finding the men at home. By 1931 there were five converts and they accompanied the missionaries when they went out preaching. In 1932 there were regular large gatherings of men each Sunday for Bible teaching from Mr. Lewis. Mrs. Lewis had a large group of children. Miss Bergsten's class for women regularly numbered in the eighties. Toward the end of 1933 the first group came forward asking for baptism.

Diasa was, perhaps, fifty years old when he came into contact with the missionaries. He spoke good Amharic and when he learned to read, the Bible became an absorbing pleasure to him. It was Diasa who first openly challenged the power of the *qalicha*, or witch doctor. At a funeral, Diasa was attempting to comfort the mourners when Gotcha Godo,[1] perhaps the most powerful qalicha at that time, interrupted. Gotcha took up the ritual pose for the curse, the long, uncut nail of his forefinger buried in the ground, the other fingers pointing at Diasa. Within six months Diasa was to die. Diasa retorted, that, if he died, then the people might well fear the power of Gotcha; but, if at the end of six months he was still alive, then let them become Christians.

The six months passed, their completion coinciding with the feast of Maskal, the great feast of the Orthodox church calendar, celebrating the finding of the cross. All over the country bonfires are lit to remind the people of the way in which the fire kindled on a hilltop had sent up a pillar of smoke which billowed along the ground until it finally reached the place where the original three crosses were buried.

But the Wallamo people did not primarily celebrate this event. Maskal is connected with their own annual sacrifice to the spirits. The celebration is partly a fertility rite, coming at the end of the rainy season,[2] but including the sacrifice of an ox. It was at the great Maskal gathering that Diasa presented himself to the people, reminding them of Gotcha's threat. It is possible that this confrontation—this challenge to the power of the qalicha, witnessed by Desta, another believer, and by Mrs. Lewis—may have marked the first real break in the power of the qalicha in Wallamo.

Walter Ohman came into Soddu in December 1933 for council meetings, after which he was due for furlough. He and Mr. Lewis examined the sixteen candidates for baptism. The missionaries re-

1. *Godo* in the Wallamo language is equivalent to *geta* in Amharic, and may be translated "master."
2. See Petros Tekle, "The Maskala" in the *Bulletin of the Ethnological Society*, 2, no. 1 (1961). It is possible that the Maskal feast in Ethiopia is a Christian rationalization of a pagan ritual.

jected three. But then, unexpectedly, the candidates suggested that they should examine one another. The missionaries could not know the significance of certain tribal customs, nor were they entirely free in the Wallamo language, so they consented to the second examination.

The matter of circumcision was raised. The ceremony is accompanied by much immorality, but it determines a man's status within the tribe. When a man dies, if he has been circumcised the grave is dug first vertically and then a horizontal shelf is excavated in which the body is laid. Sometimes a bamboo mat is placed over the opening to the shelf so that no earth might fall on the body. But if the man is uncircumcised, the body is simply placed at the bottom of the grave and the earth heaped on it. Three of the candidates who appeared to have an attitude of compromise toward the circumcision rites were disqualified by the other candidates. Thus eventually eight men and two women were the first Wallamos to be baptized.

On December 10 the baptism took place in a large pit on the mission compound. Mr. Ohman and Mr. Lewis immersed the candidates, Ato Diasa; Ato Desta and his wife Mamite; Ato Biru, who had accompanied the pioneer party of missionaries and later became leader of the Wallamo church; Wandaro, beaten and imprisoned for his faith in later years; Godana, still a leader of the Wallamo church in the seventies; Ato Cheramo and his wife Pakarei; Ato Arebo; and Kowna Cubba.[3] So, almost exactly a year after the first baptismal service in Sidamo, came the first baptismal service in Wallamo.

Two weeks later the first communion service was held. As in Sidamo a year previously, unleavened bread and honey water was used. Following this service Desta, Diasa and Godana were elected as elders. And the church was beginning to develop its own pattern of worship. The church building was erected in the usual Wallamo style, using the usual pattern of communal labor but without the traditional beer drinking. No attempt was made to translate English hymns; the believers adapted the Wallamo antiphonal singing, wedded to a five-note scale. There were no musical instruments. There were no seats in the church, but fresh grass was

3. The name *Kowna* indicates that he claimed descent from the Wallamo kings who trace their origins to Tigre province in northern Ethiopia.

Building a church in Wallamo

spread on the mud floor each Sunday. Men sat on one side of the church, women on the other.

At the meeting of the SIM field council held at Soddu from December 1 to 6, two fundamental questions were raised. The decisions made on these issues have in a measure shaped the relationship between mission and church ever since. The first concerned the location and management of a training school for evangelists. The second concerned the funds for building churches.

Mr. Street was anxious to begin training evangelists in some central location and the council discussed his proposal:

> The consensus of opinion seemed to be that a native ministry was best trained by those who had been instrumental in leading out the believers from darkness into light. This would ordinarily be by those missionaries at the station nearest the convert. Establishing a central school for such training, involving the convert's residence and a specially designated teacher, would seem to us to create an air of professionalism and an artificial barrier between the pupils and their fellows which we would seek to avoid. We believe that most of the training for evangelists should come from the assembly of God's children. After-

wards, when the church is established, we believe that if a **Bible Training Institute** for evangelists is decided upon, that it should come from the native church itself, and not as an extraneous development.

In saying this we quite understand that we are going contrariwise to almost all teaching practice of the denominational missions, but we see where they all tended to modernism and a dead orthodoxy. Even faith missions can make the same mistake. While not desiring to compare our natural wisdom with these, yet we do believe that a truer, more evangelical teaching can be developed in the assembly, rather than with the seminary idea, with its almost inevitable exaltation of wisdom.

While we thus state our earnest convictions we would like to add that we recognize our own inexperience, and in no sense wish to stand in the light of criticizing others, or policies that God may have revealed to others. We do believe that without the constant daily guidance of the Holy Spirit we are sure to make mistakes, but we do trust and believe that He has led us to these conclusions.

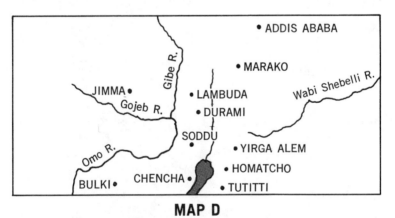

MAP D
SIM IN ETHIOPIA—1933

In fact the general lines of policy outlined here have been maintained by the mission and not until 1965 was a centrally located Bible Training Institute opened, at Jimma. But Bible schools at each mission station in the south have long been the principal means of training pastors and evangelists.

Next at the Soddu council meetings came the question of building and financing churches:

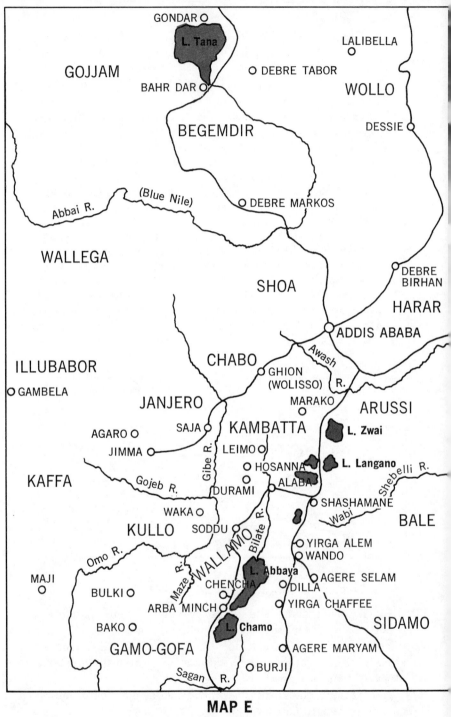

MAP E
SOUTH AND CENTRAL ETHIOPIA

At the meeting of Field Council, December 2, 1933, the matter of having church buildings conforming to indigenous church principles was discussed—the immediate cause of this discussion being the commencement of such a building, using some school funds from native sources. It was felt that this was not the right method, but that churches should be built by believers themselves, and used for the purpose of houses of worship, and moneys expended should not be mixed with school money or other funds. That the missionaries might help, but it was not thought best that they provide the money, or even a great part of it, but rather that it come from the believers themselves. It was directed that we inform the believers at Wallamo of our opinions and beliefs in the hope that they would go on themselves in confidence and dependence upon God and complete the erection of the building, the foundations of which have already been laid, and that in the future we seek to conform more strictly to these principles of indigenous church building, which we so earnestly believe in.

Here again, right at the beginning of the work, an important and easily misunderstood principle was laid down: church buildings must be of the type suited to the congregation. There are thus no sham-Gothic cathedrals or pseudo-Methodist chapels in the Ethiopian southlands. The churches are simply the usual style houses, sometimes larger than the usual home, originally thatched, now often with a corrugated iron roof. And they have been built by the believers, not by the missionaries.

It was the end of another year. There had been the first two baptismal services and the first churches had been built. In addition to the three-pronged work in Addis Ababa consisting of headquarters, leprosarium and bookshop, there were ten down-country mission stations. Homatcho and Yirga Alem to its north and Tutitti to the south. Soddu had formed the base for the advance into Gamo-Gofa with stations at Chencha and Bulki. To the west was Jimma. Over in Kambatta there were Lambuda and Durami and Marako as a staging post to the capital. See map D. Fifty-eight missionaries were at work with the SIM in Ethiopia. Four were on furlough and the Rhoads were in the States deputizing for the Binghams. Two missionaries had resigned, and two had laid down their lives.

7

The North Country
1934

On February 6, 1934 Dr. Bingham arrived in Addis Ababa with six new missionaries, including his own niece, Miss Blair, who was a registered nurse and the first member of his family to follow his steps into missionary work. A meeting of the field council was arranged for February 8-12 and at this meeting Bingham announced the resignation of George Rhoad from the mission. There had been disagreement between Dr. Lambie and Mr. Rhoad while the two men had led the work in Ethiopia, and this disagreement had been continued while Rhoad was in America acting as deputy general director. The home council had become concerned over what they were told of disaffection among the missionaries, of severe privation, even starvation of the missionaries, and of mission stations opened without proper written agreements being first concluded.

At the meeting of council these matters and others were touched upon lightly, but Bingham was obviously anxious to talk with the missionaries and to visit the stations before settling anything. It was decided that Dr. Bingham should accompany Lambie on a trip north to investigate the possibility of opening mission work in Lalibella, and then to visit the southern stations. In the meantime Malcolm Forsberg, newly arrived from America, was appointed to Chencha and Mr. and Mrs. Anderson to Bulki. The three were to travel together down to Soddu and to leave as soon as they could. The Ohmans were back in Bulki by this time, following their furlough.

74

The trip north followed an extraordinary request from Ras Kassa, governor of Lasta province, that the mission move into Lalibella. This was a new departure for the mission, for Lalibella was and still is a center of worship for the Orthodox church. In the twelfth century one of the Zagwe dynasty, the Emperor Lalibella, is believed to have begun the building of churches carved out of the sandstone rock at Roha. The place lost its old name and was renamed after the Emperor and became very much a shrine of Orthodoxy. But Ras Kassa was anxious to have the mission in the north as well as in the south and he put his proposal to Lambie in writing. On February 23 Lambie and Bingham set out.

James Luckman drove them out on the trail over Entoto mountain by car. The mule caravan had gone on ahead five days earlier. For the next three weeks they skirted the great gash in the Gojjam plateau which is the Blue Nile gorge, plunging down into the canyons through which poured some of the tributaries to the great river. They passed Magdala where Lord Napier's expedition to release Emperor Theodore's European prisoners confronted Theodore's army and where Theodore himself committed suicide. And so to Lalibella. The senior priest there welcomed them, al-

The Blue Nile Gorge

though, as Lambie had anticipated, the priests in general were far from pleased to see the missionaries. As coffee was served to them, Hiruy, the priest, asked Lambie for advice about what he took to be headache medicine. He handed the sticks over to Lambie who discovered to his astonishment that the medicine was, in fact, dynamite!

The governor of Lalibella sent a man with the missionaries to assist in selecting a site. Once a suitable place was chosen, he assured them that it would be granted to the mission without difficulty. So they headed west to Debre Tabor where Ras Kassa's eldest son, Wond-Wossen, welcomed them and discussed the possibility of opening mission stations there and at Gondar, to the north. Without finalizing anything there, they continued westward to the shores of Lake Tana, source of the Blue Nile or Abbai River and then trekked southward, crossed the Blue Nile (losing two mules by drowning in the process), and so on to Bahr Dar and Debre Markos where Ras Imru, cousin of the Emperor lived. Of him Dr. Lambie writes:

> He was, in my opinion, after the Emperor himself, the very finest man in Ethiopia. Honest and faithful to his friends, he never took a bribe or concealed a fault; he was generous and unselfish. In the war he proved himself the best general of all.[1]

Lambie suggested to Ras Imru that if a mission station were opened at Debre Markos the many blind people in the area could be helped by being taught to make baskets. Suitable willow trees grew abundantly right through the area. It was finally agreed that the SIM should open work at Debre Markos, Bahr Dar, Gondar and Lalibella. In fact the first and last were opened before the Italian occupation but war prevented anything being done then, either at Bahr Dar or at Gondar.

Mrs. Lambie was ill. Ras Imru had a radio transmitter and he agreed to ask for the Emperor's plane to be flown down to take her to Addis Ababa. But when the aircraft arrived it proved to have room for all three missionaries, who were back in the capital after a mere eighty minutes, a contrast to the two-week trek which the men had anticipated. It was early April. Almost at once Dr.

1. Thomas A. Lambie, *A Doctor's Great Commission*, p. 222.

Bingham was on the road again, this time to attend a meeting of the missionaries from the Sidamo area at Homatcho.

Briefly Bingham explained the reason for his visit and outlined the history of the relationship between the SIM and the Abyssinian Frontiers Mission. The missionaries were obviously perplexed by the reports that they were "starving," although they admitted that allowances had been low. But food available locally was inexpensive and, they insisted, nourishing. Cliff Mitchell moved that a vote of confidence in Dr. Lambie as field director be given, and this was unanimously approved. The next two days were spent with Dr. Bingham in Bible study. The day after the gathering ended, Bingham set off for a similar meeting scheduled for April 28 at Soddu.

At Soddu there was an even larger gathering of missionaries. Beside Dr. Bingham, sixteen of the workers from Wallamo, Sidamo and Kambatta met. Bingham reported first on his trip into the north, assuring the conference that there was no intention of weakening the work in the south. Next he moved on to the various criticisms voiced about the conduct of mission affairs. A very full resolution expressing confidence in the mission was proposed by Mr. Lewis and seconded by Mr. Roke:

1. We affirm our united confidence in Dr. Lambie as our Field Director. We are convinced that the reports concerning an impending secession of a number of workers from the mission on account of dissatisfaction with his administration are entirely groundless. We want it known that he continues to have our loving and prayerful support.
2. We also assure Dr. Bingham and the Home Staff of our confidence and our wholehearted approval of their administration.
3. So long as there is unoccupied territory in the line of march, with open doors through which to advance; and so long as there are fully approved and trained workers fitted to meet the need in these fields, and having their passage and outfit supplied; and so long as there is not some indication, aside from the shortage in allowances, that Christ would have us hold back for a little in carrying out His great commission to make disciples of all the nations; it is our conviction that we should go forward in the face of greater difficulties than we have faced heretofore.

Bingham returned to the capital and then traveled down to Jimma to meet with the missionaries working in the Kaffa area. Again there was a report on the trip to the north. Bingham mentioned the availability in Debre Markos of buildings suitable for missionary homes. One, built as a banqueting hall, was reported to have walls three or four feet thick. Once again the matter of mission leadership was discussed. And again the missionaries indicated their agreement with the work of Dr. Lambie and with the faith principle, which guaranteed them no fixed salary. A unanimous vote of confidence in Dr. Lambie as field director was passed.

And so back to Addis Ababa. Dr. Bingham was still concerned with the criticism that stations were opened without first obtaining written agreements. Lambie took Dr. Bingham to meet Addison Southard, the American Minister in Addis Ababa. Southard was sympathetic. He explained that Sir Sydney Barton, the British minister, had been trying unsuccessfully for five years to get a title deed for the British legation property. The Americans had no written agreement for their rented property, either. He concluded by saying, "I don't think that Dr. Lambie should be criticized for his failure when we legations fail to do what we attempt."

Reassured, Dr. Bingham left Ethiopia. But before he went he dropped a chance remark which was almost prophetic. He suggested to Lambie that it might prove necessary for someone in the mission to take Ethiopian citizenship to assure the country of the mission's wholehearted committal to her welfare.

On May 14 Mr. and Mrs. Oglesby, who had been working temporarily at the leprosarium, set off for Lalibella with Dr. Harriet Skemp and Miss Blair, Bingham's niece. Soon letters began to arrive in Addis Ababa in a steady stream, telling of their difficulties. The land selected by Dr. Lambie, and supposedly belonging to Ras Kassa, was claimed by someone else. The missionaries were living in squalid conditions in the town. The priests resented their presence, children were forbidden to attend the Sunday school, adults had been threatened with excommunication if they frequented the mission. Lambie scarcely knew where to turn to solve the problem which revived again the earlier criticisms of his failure to negotiate agreements.

No one seemed able to help. Ras Kassa promised another site, but he did not feel obliged to do anything so long as the missionaries in Lalibella had a place to live, even though it was unsatisfactory. Bilaten Geta Hiruy was sympathetic but vague. Perhaps with Dr. Bingham's words lingering in his memory Lambie said to the foreign minister:

> I cannot understand these delays and failures. You have known me for many years, and if I have let you down or wronged Ethiopia I will let you judge. I love Ethiopia and hope to spend the rest of my life serving her, and if necessary would become an Ethiopian myself to prove the sincerity of my love.

The next day Lambie was summoned to an interview with the foreign minister, who assured him that if he became an Ethiopian citizen the problems at Lalibella would disappear.

Lambie was on the brink of a trip to Jimma to investigate the chance of opening a new station at nearby Agaro. He asked for a month to think over the implications of such a step. His wife was convinced that it would not be wise for her. Others scoffed at the very idea. All through the negotiations over the Agaro work and the search for a new location for the work in Jimma, Lambie was weighing up the arguments for and against taking Ethiopian citizenship. On November 1 he returned to the capital with his mind made up. He went back to the foreign minister and announced his decision. Before the Emperor, Dr. Lambie took the oath of allegiance and so became an Ethiopian citizen.[2]

On December 5 the Italians claimed Ethiopia's Wal-Wal territory as part of Italian Somaliland. They refused to settle the boundary dispute peacefully and exaggerated the incident to major proportions as a pretext for their plans to annex Ethiopia. Understandably perturbed, Ethiopian citizen Dr. Lambie left Addis Ababa again on the day after Christmas to make a second trip to Lalibella. But this trip was more successful than the first. Traveling by way of Dessie he reached Lalibella quickly and was able to secure new land, to finalize the land contract and to see the work of building begun by the missionaries, the first party having been reinforced by Luckman and Mr. Nystrom.

2. In this way he became a "doctor without a country," as he entitled one of his books, when Ethiopia was annexed by Italy. Since Lambie's wife had retained her American citizenship he was eventually able to regain his.

While in the north he took the opportunity of traveling to Sokota, a place he had long wished to visit because of its connection with a certain Sheikh Zacharias. This Moslem was converted through a vision and then he acquired an Arabic Bible. Many of his Moslem neighbors were converted when he preached to them. He would not ally himself with the Orthodox church and became an object of persecution. Eventually he was taken to Addis Ababa and tried before Emperor Menelik who gave him a paper permitting him to carry on his work among the Moslems. So he preached. Lambie estimates that as many as five thousand may have been converted through his ministry. When Zacharias died, a man named Yusuf succeeded him and once again the persecution began. Menelik was dead and the paper he had given to Zacharias was no longer respected. Yusuf came to the capital and told his story to Dr. Lambie, asking his assistance in gaining the ear of the regent. Lambie promised to try. He was expecting the British minister and the regent for lunch on a certain day. This must have been at some time in 1924 or 1925:

> His Highness came in great state, with a retinue of perhaps two thousand who, of course, stayed outside. Luncheon went off very well, the conversation turning on such Christian subjects as whether or not we should know one another in heaven. After luncheon, while sipping our black coffee, I asked His Highness if he would consent to see a certain person as a favour to me. Ordinarily, of course, I would never think of breaking in on a social visit in this way, but I thought this was a matter of such importance that I would even risk the royal disfavour in such a cause. He graciously consented. The writ of tolerance, bearing Menelik's seal, and written on a sheep-skin parchment, was produced and examined, and Yusef questioned. Then, taking my courage in my two hands, I said to the Regent: "Your Highness, these men may not be Christians in your sense or in mine, but I believe them to be real followers of Jesus Christ. If you can do anything to help them I believe it would be pleasing to God."
>
> "I can and I will," was his earnest reply. Summoning his chamberlain he gave a few orders which resulted in Yusuf's getting what he wanted and in his being able to return to Sokota rejoicing. I was able to give him a quantity of good literature that had been sent me from the Nile Mission Press. Before leaving he gave me an earnest appeal for missionaries to come and help them.

But Lambie was unable to send missionaries to Sokota. One night as Yusuf was returning from a meeting, he was shot and killed. Now, at last, Lambie had the opportunity to visit Sokota:

> We found it to be a large town. The Governor, a blind old man, received us gladly and offered to make a place for our mission there if we would come. The little flock of believers had been decimated and were sorely in need of help. We promised ourselves that we would try to start some work there the next year. Alas, it was too late! The war came on. We never got back.

The Lambies retraced their steps to Lalibella and then continued the long trek southward. Somewhere in Gojjam province, to the south of Lake Tana, the party was met by a messenger from the mission in Addis Ababa, bearing a sack of letters and papers. They sat down on the bare hillside to read their mail, and there they were stunned by the news that their only son, Wallace, had been killed instantly in Puerto Rico where he was employed by the National City Bank. Immensely saddened, the Lambies struggled through three more weeks until they reached Addis Ababa. There Lambie saw the Emperor: "He said no word for the space of five minutes, while the tears coursed down his cheeks in sympathy with us. It meant far more than words."[3]

3. The information in this chapter comes primarily from the minutes of the meetings held at Addis Ababa, Homatcho, Soddu and Jimma, and from Dr. Lambie's book *A Doctor's Great Commission*. Rev. George Rhoad later formed the Gospel Forwarding Mission, functioning principally in the northern frontier district of Kenya.

8

War

On his way back from that second trip to Lalibella, Lambie paused at Debre Markos where he found Nick Simponis, ill with dysentery and waiting for someone to negotiate a site for the mission. Ras Imru talked the matter over with Lambie and then gave the mission a piece of land at Wonke which had belonged to Ras Hailu whose property had all been confiscated following his implication in a revolt headed up by Lij Eyasu.[1] Simponis moved onto the property and one of the two houses already on the land became his home. In May he was joined by Mr. and Mrs. Don Davies and Jean Cable who was trained in work with the blind. She was to commence the work among the blind as agreed with Ras Imru.

But in Addis Ababa it was becoming evident that war with Italy was imminent. The Lambies were due to visit England and America for the SIM in May; and, before they left, the Emperor had confided his fears of war to Dr. Lambie. Lambie had suggested that it would be good to have Red Cross work organized in good time. Although he seemed in favor of it, the Emperor would not commit himself. But in England Dr. Lambie interested some of his friends in organizing Red Cross work for Ethiopia. Then he traveled to America where he received a message from the Emperor, ordering him back to Ethiopia.

Lambie decided to fly from America to Britain with Dr. Bingham and then on to Marseilles to join Clarence Duff and Dr. Rolls from the Auckland Bible Institute on the *Berengaria*. Lambie had a rough passage in the plane. When Dr. Bingham tried

1. The successor of Emperor Menelik II, deposed by the church and succeeded by Zauditu and then Haile Sellasie I

to comfort the airsick Lambie with "Let not your heart be troubled," Lambie could only wheeze back miserably, "It's not my heart, it's my stomach!" Duff was returning from a three-month furlough which had followed a first term of service of seven and a half years. He was anxious to get back before war shut him out of Ethiopia.

On September 20 the party reached Addis Ababa. Shortly afterward Lambie was appointed executive secretary of the Ethiopian Red Cross. He called a meeting of the SIM field council where he reported,

> In view of the catastrophe that has come upon our country in the Italian war and invasion, and because the Government has appointed me Secretary Executive of the Ethiopian Red Cross; and because it has seemed to me that it is indeed God's will for me to accept this appointment; and because this takes nearly all my time; I feel that I should delegate to others most of the direction of the Mission.
>
> I therefore appoint Messrs. Duff and Cain to be Deputy Field Directors. The former to be in Addis Ababa, to care for such duties as would ordinarily be mine here . . . Mr. Cain to be in charge of all such activities as would ordinarily be mine when out of Addis Ababa.
>
> In making these appointments it is understood that I do not relinquish my work as Field Director absolutely, but that I have the right to exercise a general oversight of the work.

At the height of its activities the Red Cross had sixteen medical units operating, number four being an all-SIM contribution. On October 3, 1935 Italian forces under General de Bono crossed the Mareb River and invaded Ethiopia. Rebellion flared at Debre Markos where the acting governor ordered Miss Cable back to the capital. Mrs. Davies had been ill and she and her husband had already left, but Simponis was not alone for long: the Cains and Jack Starling arrived on the last day of 1935 with some seventy mules for the British Red Cross unit to the north. They found Simponis living in the town where he had withdrawn on the order of the governor. The following day a pitched battle was fought across the mission property and the rebels appeared to be the victors. However they failed to follow up their success by occupying the town and the governor's forces were afforded a breathing space to regroup. The missionaries were soon engaged in treating the wounded, hundreds of whom were brought into the town for them to deal with. They were living in tents but were anxious to have permanent buildings up on their property so that, if the Italians came in, they would find a work already under way and might permit it to continue. Toward the middle of January, government forces appeared to have regained the initiative, and Cain and Simponis started building on the Wonke site. But they were not allowed to remain there, even when the buildings were habitable; understandably the governor did not want foreigners isolated from the town. Four times Debre Markos was bombed, and the missionaries did their best to cope with the scores of injured.

In the south the fighting was not going well. The Red Cross units suffered too. On December 20 the Swedish unit was attacked from the air; an ambulance driver, Mr. Lundstrom was killed and Dr. Hylander was wounded. The SIM Red Cross unit found it no easy task to get their two trucks across the Arussi desert to the front. At Yirga Alem they abandoned the trucks and went on with mules and, later still, camels. In Negelli[2] they were bombed and left stranded by their guides. Making a fresh start with their trucks they finally reached Ras Desta's forces which were already in retreat. Ras Desta retreated with them, but later in the retreat the trucks had to be abandoned. Salvaging what they could, the missionaries pressed northward on mules. Dr. Hooper, at sixty-two still amazingly fit, was flown back to Addis Ababa from Yirga Alem in a Red Cross plane.

The missionaries from Tutitti, Homatcho and Yirga Alem met at the provincial capital to decide what to do. It seemed best for Tom Devers and Allen Smith to remain at Yirga Alem. Alan Webb would go with Mr. and Mrs. Mitchell, Mr. and Mrs. Alf Roke, Miss MacGregor and Miss Pogue, Tom Dever's fiancée, to the capital, and try to get medical supplies together for a new venture. On February 12 the party arrived in Addis Ababa, the first of many that would arrive over the months ahead. At once Webb set about assembling supplies for a return to Sidamo. With Cliff Mitchell he made two unsuccessful forays, blocked each time by rain-swollen rivers. The third time they traveled on mules and March 18 saw them clear of Addis Ababa.

2. Negelli in Borana, not Negelli in Arussi.

Back again at Yirga Alem they decided that, while Cliff Mitchell and Tom Devers remained on the station, Allen Smith and Alan Webb would help Dr. Roberts in his Red Cross work. In April Tom Devers traveled across to Soddu to discuss plans with Ray Davis, a very close friend. They agreed on where they might meet so that they could make the trip to Addis Ababa together, if necessary. And Tom entrusted a package to Mr. Davis. In it was his Bible and his ring, to be given to his fiancée if Ray Davis reached Addis Ababa first or if anything should happen to Tom. Devers returned to Yirga Alem.

But now law and order were breaking down everywhere. In January Mr. Street and Mr. John Trewin at Chencha were arrested and imprisoned. After a couple of days they were released but were rearrested on two further occasions. On one occasion Mr. Street was actually chained, one report adding that his own dog chain was used, gratuitous rudeness if true, since the epithet *wisha* (dog) is an extreme insult. News of this reached the authorities in Addis Ababa and orders were at once sent down for the release of the men. From the end of February the little party at Shamma, just outside Chencha, was left alone. But in April the district was in uproar with inter-tribal fighting, slave-raiding and wholesale murder. Threats to pillage the mission station and to carry off the Street children added to the anxieties of the missionaries, but they were unable to obtain mules to make the trip to the comparative safety of Soddu.

In May they received word from Clarence Duff, in charge in Addis Ababa, that missionaries should not attempt to travel around, but remain quietly on their stations. The message reached them through Walter Ohman at Soddu, and he also relayed the message to Yirga Alem, but the message probably failed to reach them. The five men at Yirga Alem discussed the situation. Dr. Roberts and Alan Webb decided to go to Soddu. Allen Smith joined the Norwegian Red Cross unit operating in Sidamo and remained with it until it withdrew to Kenya. Cliff Mitchell had his wife and baby in Addis Ababa, and Tom Dever's fiancée was there. They decided to try to reach the capital. On May 7 the two men left Yirga Alem with a party of some twenty others. They headed across the Kassai desert to cross the Bilate river at a point which marks the confluence of Sidamo, Arussi, Wallamo, and

Kambatta tribes. On the afternoon of May 9 they were attacked by a mob of some two hundred Arussi Gallas, and the entire party was massacred.

Shortly afterward a party of Ethiopian soldiers came across the scene of the tragedy, and the news was telephoned to Soddu from Negelli. It reached them on May 15.

In Addis Ababa Dr. Lambie was awakened a little after midnight on the night of May 1 by the sound of a car horn. It was Dejazmatch Biru, making his final appearance in this story. The Lambies had cared for his daughter, Taferta Sellassie, since she was born on January 23, 1934. Now Biru wanted her with him as he traveled with the Emperor to Jibouti and to exile. At about a quarter past three in the morning the missionaries heard the mournful whistle of the departing train as it left Addis Ababa.

The interval before the arrival of the Italians on May 5 was filled with looting, banditry, and murder. All foreigners had long before been advised to leave the country, but the missionaries did not feel it was right to walk out just when they might be able to help. Dr. Bingham had cabled:

> You are under higher orders than those of the King of England or the President of the United States. Get your instructions from Him, and we are one with you. We approve the sending home of mothers with children.

The missionaries all decided to stay; and, when the crisis came, they felt it unfair to expect the embassies to protect them. They gathered at the headquarters building, four men and sixteen women and children. Barbed wire was set up around the compound: someone poked a nozzle of a hosepipe over the wall with the thought that it might look like some kind of weapon. Occasionally one of the men fired off one of the two rifles and two shotguns which were on the property, hoping that the noise might prove a deterrant to raiders.

The mission's Ethiopian employees were unsure what to do, fearful to remain with the missionaries who might attract looters, but fearful also to trust the roads. Lambie spoke to them:

> Did I ever lie to you? Well, I am going to say now that the same God who said to Paul that He had given him all the lives with him on the shipwrecked boat has spoken to me and given

me assurance that all who stay on the mission compound will, in like manner, be given to me.

They stayed and no one was hurt.

Across the other side of the city was the school for the blind, run by Miss Leona Kibby. Her home was packed with the blind beggars and priests whom she taught to read in Braille. All through the months of the invasion she had continued her teaching, but on May 2 she crossed the city to be with the other missionaries. Bruce Ostien, Harry Glover, Tommy Simpson and Dr. Lambie took turns patrolling the compound at night. Fiona MacLuckie, later to work for many years in Kambatta and now acting as Dr. Lambie's secretary, was there; and Jean Cable, Edna Smartt, Mrs. Mitchell, and Gertrude Pogue. The days passed with smoke hanging in wreaths over the city and the sound of firing almost continuous. By Tuesday morning a calm descended over the city; late in the afternoon the Italians entered. On the sixth some of the missionaries went into the city. Most of the center of the town was burned out; corpses were strewn everywhere. The big stone Bible house was almost undamaged, but the bookshop was gutted. Across the other side of the city, Miss Kibby's blind school was still intact. The cheap padlock still hung undamaged from the latch.

Dr. Lambie went to surrender to the Italian authorities. His telegram to *The Times* of London concerning the use by the Italians of mustard gas had been published in the issue of March 25, and his open condemnation of the aggression was known to the Italians. His action now, in surrendering personally, was criticized as unnecessary by some of the missionaries. Lambie, of course, based his action on Romans 13:1, "be subject to the higher powers." Rome was governing and he must be subject. Not everyone shared his phlegmatic approach.[3]

In Marako, Daisy McMillan and Freda Horn lived dangerously. The Bartons had left for furlough in September of 1934, and no

3. Least of all the Ethiopian authorities. The English term "surrender" does not exist in Amharic; nearest equivalent is *idj sette,* "he gave his hand" signifying an offer of friendship. Those who "gave the hand" to the Italians were contemptuously termed *banda,* "traitor." Haile Sellassie refused to meet Lambie in Khartoum, and yet Lambie was honestly puzzled by the emperor's hostility. Cultural barriers can be as impenetrable as this, even to men of good will.

replacement was available for them. This normally would have meant the closing of the station, but the two women asked to be allowed to remain. They continued together for some eighteen months. Two days after the departure of the Emperor from the capital, news of the events there reached Marako. At once all order broke down. Local officials fled, the prison gates were thrown open, telephone lines were cut, homes were ransacked. As darkness fell on May 6,

> Some fifty armed bandits came to the mission station. They stated that one of their number was sick. Miss Horn, who is a trained nurse,[4] tried to find out what was the matter, but it became obvious that the request for medicine was a mere pretext for entering the compound. Almost at once the men crowded into the house, striking and kicking the two women. Resistance was impossible and the missionaries meekly submitted to whatever indignities their brutal assailants chose to inflict upon them. Perhaps what hurt them most of all was to recognize amongst the mob several who were well known to them, and to whom they had preached the gospel of Jesus Christ.
>
> In fifteen minutes the robbers had practically cleared the house and destroyed or damaged whatever they could not carry away. Even doors and windows were wrenched off their hinges and the house was stripped bare. The bandits then hurried off.

It was obviously impossible for the women to remain in their own home, but they were four days journey from Addis Ababa, and throughout the area the tribes were in ferment. Ato Dembel took control. He had become a Christian ten years before the arrival of missionaries in Marako through reading the Amharic Bible. He was something of a visionary, but now he acted decisively. The two ladies went to his compound and moved into an empty hut. They were able to get a message through to the mission in Addis Ababa telling of their safety, but they could not expect any help from that direction. After a couple of weeks Ato Dembel left them alone and rode off on his mule to prepare the way for the journey to the capital.

It was no light thing to shelter foreigners at this time. One of the Armenians who lived at Marako was killed in cold blood and

4. Actually Miss Horn was not a trained nurse.

his body hacked to pieces; it is obvious that in those days a white skin was often equated with the Italian invaders.

On June 1 the two missionaries left Marako, accompanied by Ato Dembel and a few of his servants. All the way to Addis Ababa they were accompanied by relays of armed men provided by the local chiefs who had been contacted by Ato Dembel. From time to time they encountered bands of marauding tribesmen, but in spite of muttered threats to kill them, the little party made its way safely to Addis Ababa. They arrived on June 4 after a month in which death was never far away.

Up in Chencha the Streets and John Trewin were besieged. The treasury in the town was ransacked and violence threatened the mission. They decided to leave, but Miss Bray had scarcely moved off on her mule than a party of men turned her back, rifled her belongings and then marched Harold Street about the compound at gunpoint, taking whatever they fancied. That night the missionaries all slept in one house. At about 9:30 Miss Bray's house and the clinic were broken into by a mob and cleaned out. In the morning an even bigger mob appeared, but the house where the missionaries were gathered was left alone. Over the weeks the situation fluctuated. Supplies ran out. But at the end of June, mules and carriers reached them from Soddu. On July 4, through the pouring rain, they reached Soddu.

Across in Kambatta the missionaries at Durami had been advised early in the year that they should move to Hosanna. So the Cousers at Lambuda were joined by Mr. and Mrs. John Phillips and Zillah Walsh. On May 8 word of the departure of the Emperor and of the troubles in Addis Ababa reached Hosanna. Again chaos ensued. Kambattans and the Hadya people joined the Gallas in an attack on the Amhara. In the early hours of the morning the missionaries packed what they could and took refuge in the woods. The following evening they returned to Lambuda, but on May 10, with fighting spreading, they left again. Their homes were ransacked. Fitawrari Belachew promised them that if they returned they would be protected and some, at least, of their stolen goods would be restored. But when they returned they were disheartened by what they found: food trampled into the floor, books torn to shreds, the little harmonium smashed. They passed the night under canvas in the woods.

Eventually Belachew agreed to let them settle on the compound of Grazmatch Tekettele. On May 14 word reached them that the Catholic mission station at Wasero had been sacked and the two missionaries killed. Only later did they learn that, in fact, one of the missionaries recovered.

Four days later the grazmatch retreated to Hosanna town and a threatening mob surrounded his compound. When the situation appeared most dangerous, Ato Gadicho, one of the believers, arrived with an escort of men who forced their way through the mob and led the missionaries to his own home. Three days later they moved again, to Gadicho's brother's house. On his compound they were given a hut to live in. In his diary John Phillips recalls, "At dusk we had rather a hard rain which enabled us to locate the worst leaks!"

On May 29 they moved into yet another house. The occupants were fifteen people, five or six horses, six cows and their calves, a dog or two and a rooster. Despite the conditions they could say, "We have much indeed for which to praise the Lord in this new situation." But they were not entirely cut off. Pur Mohammed, the Indian trader in Hosanna in whose home the first missionaries had taken refuge back in 1928, sent word of their plight to Soddu and promised to try also to get word through to Duff in Addis Ababa. He was unsuccessful in this, but on June 23 the fugitives heard that Dejazmatch Makonnen at Soddu was trying to bring the chaos in Kambatta to an end.

They moved again in order to be near some of the Christians from Dubancho. It was there that they heard from Ato Shibashi of the sacking of the Durami mission station. On Sunday August 2 they watched a pitched battle between Amhara and Moslem forces. While the fighting was still going on, they watched a Moslem woman carrying the dead from the battlefield. Although fired on, she removed some thirty corpses.

The weeks passed, the sound of the distress call going up almost continually, although no help could be expected. When news of the murder of the Catholic missionary reached Dejazmatch Makonnen he sent word across to the officials in Hosanna warning them of the consequences if the SIM workers were harmed. So the missionaries were called into Hosanna where, in spite of the threats of the soldiers, they were given refuge in one of the shops.

It was September 9. The five missionaries and one wee baby had been fugitives since May 9.

A month later soldiers escorted them to Soddu. Some of the Kambatta Christians insisted on going along with them. Abba Gole, later a leader of the church for some forty years, went along in search of his wife who had been carried off during the fighting in Kambatta. Ato Shigute, one of the first converts from Kambatta, was another.

In the north the Italian advance had been swift. In April they were in Debre Markos and the Cains, with Jean Cable were sent off to Addis Ababa, leaving Mr. Simponis and Jack Starling behind. Mr. Starling had been waylaid by shiftas.[5] They had demanded money and he was not willing to hand it over. As he sat on his horse, looking into ten rifle muzzles, a hazy recollection came to him that to stroke a man's beard was an irresistible token of friendship. He urged his horse forward and reached out to the leader of the shiftas who was:

> a great strapping fellow with a face like Mephistopheles. Reaching out my hand I seized him by the beard and stroked him beneath his chin! To my utter astonishment his face broke into a broad grin. The tension was broken and, without waiting to see what might happen next, I dug my heels into my horse and again took a chance and galloped away.

Only a month after the Cains and Miss Cable reached Addis Ababa Jack Starling was there, too, and once more Mr. Simponis was alone. The Italians informed him that he, too, would have to leave for the capital, where all missionaries were being assembled. So he checked the mission property, made an inventory of all that was being left behind and obtained receipts for it from the Italian governor.

He was flown out in an Italian aircraft, together with an Italian general. They flew first to Lake Tana, but the weather there was bad and the pilot was forced to turn back and then he was unable to locate Debre Markos because of low clouds. They made a forced landing in a field. Planes sent out to locate them were

5. The verb *shaffata* carries the meaning of abandoning a normal way of living. The *shifta* operate in groups and must not be confused with common thieves. It usually requires a military operation to clear them from a district, and they will quickly return if they are not rounded up.

contacted over the radio but were unable to find them. The next day they were spotted and an aircraft dropped two containers of aviation fuel, one of which burst when the parachute failed to open. Still they couldn't take off. That evening a smaller aircraft landed; between them they were able to get the bigger aircraft turned around and the following day they got off the ground. They flew to Asmara, then to Assab and south again to Diredawa. From there Simponis was put on the train to Addis Ababa which he finally reached on September 9.

Still further north the Oglesbys were alone at Lalibella: Mr. Nystrom had left in November 1935 for his marriage to Dr. Skemp, and in February Luckman, too, had left for Addis Ababa. From February onward a stream of war wounded was brought into the mission from Ras Kassa's army. Down in Addis Ababa, Mr. Nystrom and his wife gathered medical supplies together and set off to the relief of Mr. and Mrs. Oglesby. But they could get no further than Dessie. There they joined up with British and Dutch Red Cross units and eventually escaped from the town only hours ahead of the Italian forces who entered Dessie on April 15.

The Nystroms, incidentally, traveled out with *The Times* reporter, who had gone north with a truckload of gas masks supplied largely through the initiative of Lady Barton, wife of the British minister, and Rev. A. Matthew who was minister of the Anglican church in Addis Ababa. Back in the capital the missionaries realized that the Oglesbys were completely cut off.

On April 14, the Emperor arrived at the mission station at Lalibella, together with Ras Kassa and his two sons. Wond-Wossen was appointed governor in place of his father who was to accompany Haile Sellassie southward. Again the Oglesbys were alone. They could receive no news from the outside world and learned of the fall of Addis Ababa from papers dropped from an Italian aircraft. The pilot also required them to indicate their nationality and the nature of their work. They sent a runner into Sokota, already taken by the Italians and a week later the Italians were in Lalibella. Only a token force was sent in, and until September this force was besieged in their fort. Wond-Wossen had difficulty in maintaining order in the countryside, and only his residence on the mission compound restrained the people from sacking the place.

But in September the token force was relieved. At the end of the year Mr. Oglesby was called in by the Italian authorities and told to go to the capital to make arrangements for the closing of the work at Lalibella. On January 24 he was in Addis Ababa, discussing the situation with Duff and Cain. Two weeks later he set off back to Lalibella to arrange to close the work.

At Addis Ababa or at Soddu the missionaries were gradually assembling. In May Dr. Roberts and Alan Webb reached Soddu from Sidamo and in July the missionaries from Chencha arrived. The party from Kambatta came in on September 9. The Andersons from Bulki arrived in Soddu. The Italians came in on January 26, 1937 and occupied the town, but there was still no word of the Forsbergs who remained alone at Bulki. And Mrs. Forsberg was expecting a baby.

When the Greek traders in Gofa decided to leave, the Forsbergs felt it was time for them to leave too. The first day they left in the early evening and traveled until midnight. The second day was a long, hard pull. At daybreak on the third day they were on their way again, pausing only to gather information about conditions ahead. They rested briefly and set off at four o'clock in the afternoon, planning to travel through the night to avoid the dangers of the town of Boli. Twelve hours later they slipped through the town and camped in the early morning sunshine by the roadside. At nightfall they set off again.

Mrs. Forsberg's legs were badly swollen; she had lost the soles of her shoes and was unable to walk, even had she been fit enough to attempt to. They crossed the Demi river and were in Wallamo country. Soon after midnight they camped at "Sunday Market"[6] and so dawned the fifth day of travel on the agonizingly slow and nearly exhausted mules. They sent a messenger ahead of them and in the late afternoon a party of missionaries from Soddu came out to meet them. It was February 1937. Gamo-Gofa, too, was emptied of its missionaries.

In Addis Ababa the first party of missionaries to arrive from down-country had been the little group from Sidamo in February 1935. In June the two women from Marako came in and then the

6. A market is held on a particular day of the week. The location is then named accordingly, "Sunday market," "Tuesday market," etc.

missionaries from Debre Markos. In December Mr. Piepgrass from Jimma was ordered by the Italians to go to Addis Ababa to arrange for the closing of the work at Agaro and Jimma. In November of 1936 Mr. Shank had left Agaro for Jimma with symptoms of appendicitis. Since then the Shanks, Mr. and Mrs. Piepgrass, Irma Schneck and Mary Beam had been working together in Jimma. They hoped for a gradual return to more stable conditions, when they might reopen their work at Agaro. The Italians, however, announced the expropriation of SIM property. On December 4 the Shanks, Miss Schneck and Mr. Piepgrass went to Addis Ababa. Next month Ken Oglesby was there with the same story: the work at Lalibella must be closed.

Entries from the SIM headquarters diary tell the story of the massacres of February 1937:

> Feb. 19 This morning shooting was heard at the Gibbe. Later it was learned that the Viceroy had called the poor to the Gibbe to give gifts, on the occasion of the birth of the Prince of Naples. Ten hand grenades were thrown from the crowd, wounding about twenty Italians. The Viceroy was wounded in the leg. The chief of the Air Force had a leg taken off, and Colonel Marzie was wounded in the arm. Immediately an order was given, and natives all over the town were shot down or beaten and houses burned. The constant rattle of machine guns and clouds of smoke ascending on every side told of the tragedy which descended upon thousands of defenseless poor, who didn't even know the reason for the sudden outburst.
>
> Feb. 21 These days have been terrible beyond description; seeing innocent, frightened men shot down at the whim of the common soldier makes the heart sick. This evening the shooting is less, and it is rumoured that an order has been given to cease. Thousands are homeless without food or money, and with the winter before them.[7]

Nineteen missionaries and seven of their children were gathered at Soddu. From February onward they began to be evacuated to Addis Ababa. One of the last groups to leave was escorted by Ray

7. Ethiopia has two seasons, the rainy season from June or July to September, and the dry season. From November to January night temperatures drop to near freezing. Crops are harvested after the rainy season: to be homeless and destitute in February was calamitous.

Davis, reaching the capital on April 25. Two days later the Ogles-bys came in from their lonely outpost at Lalibella. And on the 28th the Ohmans arrived from Soddu, the last of the down-country missionaries to reach Addis Ababa.

In August Captain Bertinatti announced at a service at the Swedish mission that all mission buildings were to be expropriated and would be placed under his control. Discussion began on com-pensation. Dr. Bingham cabled instructions to Duff who was con-ducting the negotiations for the SIM: "Accept settlement for Furi[8] if payment made in pounds sterling outside of country. Stay at Akaki[9] indefinitely."

On November 2 the total price to be paid to the mission as compensation was agreed, but Duff had no written authorization to conduct the negotiations. Bingham was on his way to Australia. Duff cabled to him at Cairo and then traveled down to Jibouti to receive the necessary authorization. On December 3 he was back in Addis Ababa, but the document he brought did not satisfy the Italians: they were anxious to ensure that no legal complications would arise later.

Once more Bingham was contacted and fresh documents ar-rived for Duff from Australia. On February 5 the authorities gave notice that all the papers must be signed within a week and that on the day the signing was complete the properties must be va-cated. The missionaries managed to hold on for six months. Bing-ham appealed to the British and American governments to protest the Italian policy, but the politicians were no help.

Those months were hard on the missionaries. In small parties they left—some for home and furlough, and others, such as the Cains and the Ohmans, for a new work in the Sudan. Miss Pogue, who had been engaged to Tom Devers, had appendicitis, contacted peritonitis, and died on January 10. Harry Glover died shortly afterward.

On August 21, 1938 the last SIM missionary left. They left of their own accord. None were actually expelled, as was the case with some who represented other boards. Mr. Bevan, the represen-tative of the Bible Society in Addis Ababa, was served an expul-sion order, but his wife's name was not included. Much to the

8. Name of the hill on which the leprosarium was built.
9. The site of the mission headquarters.

dismay of the Italians, she was not at the train station when her husband left, but stayed and held the fort at the Bible house.

Mrs. Bevan expressed the feelings of the missionaries: "God is not leaving Ethiopia. He is simply changing His workmen."

9

Balance Sheet

The mission received £18,870 as compensation for their expropriated properties. Ninety-two missionaries had served with the SIM/AFM in Ethiopia. Miss Bessie Martin, Mrs. Couser, Tom Devers, Cliff Mitchell, Miss Pogue, and Harry Glover had died. Among them they appeared to have made little better than one convert each in more than ten years of labor.

In Sidamo four men had been baptized on Christmas day in 1932. A year later, on December 10, 1933 ten were baptized in Wallamo, and a second baptismal service, conducted by the believers, followed later. In Lambuda, Kambatta, there had been two baptisms before the missionaries left: one on April 22, 1934 and the second on May 14, 1935. In October 1935 Mr. Ohman and Raymond Davis were traveling through Gamo-Gofa prospecting for new stations and Mr. Ohman baptized three men, Saka, Sonkura and Simberu. At a meeting of field council from April 1 to 4, 1936, the leaders recorded their progress:

> As we review the work of the mission stations of the past few years, and survey the present situation, surrounded and accompanied as it has been by unusual difficulties and unexpected perils, we are constrained to praise the Lord and exclaim "See what God has wrought."
>
> In spite of the war which broke out last October, on ten out of fifteen stations the work of preaching and teaching has gone on to the present time, practically unhindered. Until very recently missionaries have made itinerating preaching trips in a number of the provinces in the south. When we remember that on one field twenty-six have been baptized and on another twenty-five, and lesser numbers on other stations, and that of these some

97

twenty were baptized since the war began we rejoice, give thanks, and take these victories as the pledge and promise of greater things.

The war, far from hindering the work, appeared positively to encourage it. Ato Dembel, who escorted the Marako missionaries to Addis Ababa, was baptized on June 7, 1936. In August Mr. Piepgrass reported that four had been baptized at Jimma and four more were baptized before the missionaries left Jimma in December. In September Ato Shigute and Ato Retabo, who had accompanied the refugee Kambatta missionaries to Soddu were baptized there. In November Ato Zelleke and Ato Dibbisa were baptized in Addis Ababa. When in April the missionaries left Soddu, they left behind forty-eight baptized believers.

But in July word reached them in Addis Ababa of a big baptismal service at Soddu. Twenty-three were baptized and the total was given as now seventy-three believers. This figure probably includes the two men from Kambatta. On July 18 three more Kambattans were baptized at Akaki in Addis Ababa: Ato Shibashi, Ato Desaleny and Ato Lota. The baptisms continued: Gabre-Sellassie on August 1; fourteen more reported from Wallamo on October 11; Mr. Barton's houseboy, Terrefe; on October 31. Ato Emmanuel Gabre-Sellassie led a most fruitful evangelistic campaign in the capital.

On August 29 Ato Shigute and Ato Sabiro, who had returned from Soddu to Addis Ababa with Mr. Couser, were ordained by the missionaries as elders of the Kambatta church as Clarence Duff laid his hands on them. The next day they left for Kambatta with permission to be away from their work with the missionaries for a month. The two men traveled around teaching the few believers and then they conducted their first baptismal service. Among the eight baptized believers were Abba Gole, Ato Shigute's second wife (his first wife's sister), and Ato Ababa Bushiro. After being away for six weeks, the two men returned to Addis Ababa, having first appointed Abba Gole and Ato Haile-Maryam as the first elders of the church at Dubancho. They apologized for overstaying their leave: "The work was so beautiful," they explained. Indeed, the church was growing rapidly.

Part 2: Outcome
The Church in the South
1938-1970

10

After Midnight

During the years of the Italian occupation the SIM received no news from the church in southern Ethiopia. Italian policy was to replace the Ethiopic script with the Roman script. They would not transmit materials into or out of the country unless they were written in Roman characters. Since the Ethiopian Christians could read only the Ethiopic script, the information blackout was complete.

Laurie Davison returned to Ethiopia with the British army. In May 1941 Emperor Haile Sellassie reentered his capital. Movement within the country became less restricted. Davison was placed in command of a repatriation center for Ethiopian troops in Addis Ababa. Wallamos who passed through the camp took the news of the presence of a former SIM missionary to the Wallamo people. From the Wallamo church, elders trekked up to the capital to talk with him. He began to assemble the facts, and from them the story of a miracle was told.

> Now comes the astonishing news that there are over seventy groups of believers meeting regularly for worship. In the Sidamo province Ganami has proved a faithful pastor to his flock. Ato Biru, the leading evangelist in the Wallamo area, has done a truly splendid work. He spends his time walking round the province, telling out the gospel, teaching the young Christians and preparing them for baptism.[1]

> When we left Abyssinia we had only three partly organized churches with not more than a hundred and fifty believers, but during the Italian occupation the numbers have grown by leaps and bounds, so that they estimated that there are now ten thousand believers.[2]

1. *Other Sheep for His Fold.*
2. T. A. Lambie, *A Doctor's Great Commission.*

In 1943 the Rev. G. W. Playfair, successor to Dr. R. V. Bingham as General Director of the SIM, visited the country with some missionaries. Having left only fifty baptized believers, what did they see on their return? The first report showed not less than twenty thousand rejoicing in Christ. Instead of a few scattered churches they found over three hundred.

. . . There are now found in Wallamo over 200 churches and approximately 25,000 Christians. At Kambatta there are one hundred churches and between fifteen and twenty thousand Christians. From these two areas alone the Christians have sent missionaries into other parts of the country. Their efforts have established churches in Sidamo, Kabo, Arussi, Gamo and Gofa.[3]

Coming back to the work of the churches in southern Ethiopia: this has now resolved itself into two ecclesiastical districts, Wallamo with 180 churches and Gudeila-Kambatta (usually referred to as the Kambatta district) with 100 churches.[4]

The report of Mr. L. A. Davison[5] is the most reliable of the many accounts of the situation in Wallamo following the occupa-

3. *Moving Mountains in Ethiopia.*
4. "Deputy General's Report for Ethiopia," *Sudan Witness,* 1945.
5. Unsigned, but internal evidence identifies the author.

Christians in front of their unfinished church (framework to be mudded over)

tion. In May 1945, after four years spent in postoccupation Ethiopia, and three months of careful observation of the Wallamo church at first hand, Mr. Davison wrote a report from which the following extracts are taken:

We have found here as indigenous a church as Roland Allen[6] ever dreamed about, and it is our earnest hope that no member of our mission will do or say anything to destroy the autonomous structure of this amazing Wallamo church. The membership today stands at somewhere around fifteen thousand baptized believers, and its remarkable history comes a grand second to that recorded in the book of the Acts of the Apostles.

The territory is divided into fifteen sections, with one Ruling Elder in each section. Then each section is divided into individual church areas, with four or more elders in each church. Minor matters of dispute that arise within a church are settled by the elders of the church concerned. Matters a little more difficult are referred to the Ruling Elder of the district, who may call the elders of several of his churches together and settle the matter. Matters of great importance are taken by the Ruling Elder to the Monthly Meeting, where the Council of Ruling Elders regularly considers such matters.

In the life of the Wallamo church as a whole the monthly meeting holds a very important place. Each month the meeting is held at a different place, which custom originated during the times of terrific Roman Catholic and Fascist persecution. The work has grown so large that this monthly meeting has to be restricted to not more than three or four representatives for each church. At the appointed day and place the folks begin to gather at dusk, reaching the peak about midnight. While the folks are gathering, quite a lot of social chatter is enjoyed, not without some chorus[7] singing and messages of spiritual exhortation by some of the Ruling Elders. Just before midnight the evening meal is served, and folks then settle down for the night. The Ruling Elders sleep in a separate hut, and at daybreak next morning they, the Ruling Elders, have their own special meeting to discuss the problems of the month.

When the Ruling Elders have finished their discussions they

6. He refers to Roland Allen's two missionary classics, *The Spontaneous Expansion of the Church* and *Modern Missionary Methods, St. Paul's or Ours?* Both strongly advocate indigenous principles.

7. By which he means the singing of the antiphonal hymns generated spontaneously in such gatherings.

Evening meal at the monthly meeting

move into the main church building to meet the crowds who represent the Wallamo church as a whole. The Presiding Elder is now able to make any announcements, including the fixture for the place of the next meeting, which the Council of Ruling Elders has just decided, and to have these decisions conveyed by those present to the individual churches and believers. Then follow the main spiritual and devotional messages of the Conference. Immediately afterwards breakfast follows and the assembly breaks up just about midday for another month's work. Let it be emphasized that this organization is wholly indigenous, and was built up when there was no missionary in their country to exercise what he loves to think of as his indispensable guidance to the work of God.

Matters of doctrine have not, as yet, taken much prominence in the church, but to me the indications are that this point has now been reached, all unconsciously, and I foresee the immediate need for doctrinal instruction, because matters are already arising which will, I am sure, only reach final settlement when discussion reduces them to the bed rock of the foundation truths of New Testament doctrine.

Two weeks ago I was able to attend a baptismal service some distance from here. I insisted on going only as an observer. The service is simple. The method is immersion and the after meeting is a communion service. It is worth mentioning here that although even at a wedding of believers all the old practices of feasting or dancing, or in fact any outward expression of joy, is banned, yet at a baptism this ban is lifted. Even though baptisms occur only on Sundays, singing and rejoicing and even horse sports (a thing very dear to the heart of every true Wallamo), is allowed in the procession to and from the river. This remarkable rejoicing at a baptism service is doubtless a very deep-rooted and probably unconscious carry-over of the old tribal idea of the enlargement of the clan.

Once a month communion is observed throughout all the churches simultaneously, the time being set at the Monthly Meeting. The service, which is known as "Eating the secret", is observed very early in the morning. . . . The elements consist of simple native bread made by a carefully chosen house-mother, and the wine is literally honey-water. The elements are served by the church pastor, assisted by his elders.

Ministry Under this heading we come to the most needy field in this church today. Church government is not OUR problem at all. . . . But the need for Bible instruction amongst the pastors is appalling. All the Wallamo scriptures we have been able to place in their hands has been an edition of St. John's Gospel, numbering just under a thousand. . . . Hence the people and pastors have to depend on Amharic scriptures. We have been able to distribute many thousands of Bibles and portions in this language. . . . Most of the pastors are handicapped in more ways than language. Some have great difficulty in reading. Many have great difficulty in changing the Amharic text into their own mother-tongue. So much so that when they are through it has lost its true meaning altogether. Most have so little Bible perspective and grip upon the historical, geographical and spiritual background of the scriptures that their interpretation of isolated passages is often regrettably distorted.

Then, too, such a memorandum as this would not be complete without some reference to Ato Biru, who is undoubtedly the leader of the whole Wallamo church. Biru's character as a man is above reproach. He has a dynamic, fanatical way of public address when aroused by opposition, but his normal sermons are rambling and lacking in clear thought or spiritual food. He deals mostly in platitudes and negatives. Herein lies his chief weakness, and many of his contemporaries, some of whom were reborn out of his testimony, have far outgrown him in spiritual leadership. Nevertheless, the Wallamo church, without a doubt, grew up around Biru, and he is therefore treated with veneration by all concerned. At Council meetings and even in public meetings, he usually displays a domineering spirit and insists emphatically upon having the last word in all matters. He is obviously very jealous to maintain his own prestige. He cherishes the hope of one day building a stone "temple" with a corrugated iron roof where his present church stands, in order to surpass all the other Wallamo churches. Immediately after the overthrow of the Italians he encouraged the believers to begin the building of this temple at which time he was in the hey-day of his fame. The Amharic[8] authorities providentially put a stop to this before the foundations were laid! However, it is amazing how much material was gathered and is still lying about outside the present church.

Before Messrs. Playfair and Roke appointed fifteen elders to assist him, Biru was forced to make many important decisions alone,[9] and I personally feel that he is to be most highly commended for the way in which he moulded and guided in the formation of the infant church in those early years of its fastest growth. Because of this I feel that, although we deplore some of his characteristics, we must uphold his authority and support his leadership, while at the same time we may seek gradually to transfer the final word of authority to the Council of Ruling Elders.

This was the Wallamo church. To the north lay the only slightly smaller Kambatta church and already, to the south, was the nucleus of the Gamo-Gofa church. This explosive and spontaneous expansion of the church had covered a span of but a few years. It is interesting to see how these developments came about in the absence of the missionaries.

8. Amharic is the language spoken by the Amhara people.
9. Actually Mr. Playfair, successor as general director of the SIM to Dr. Bingham, did not appoint the fifteen elders, but advised the seven hundred or so elders who met with him on his visit to Wallamo in July 1943 that the number of elders should be increased to fifteen.

11

Linguistic Interlude

The church which is now spread throughout southern Ethiopia has spread from three inter-dependent foci, Wallamo, Kambatta and Sidamo. These three are, in fact, the three areas into which the SIM was first led in 1928. From Wallamo the church has expanded southward into Gamo-Gofa and westward into Kullo-Konta. From Kambatta extension has been westward to Janjero and eastward toward Arussi. From Sidamo the movement has been southward to Darassa and down into Burji where it has linked up with the southern outreach of Wallamo. It is highly significant that the expansion has been checked to the north of Shashamane, to the east of Sidamo, to the west of Kullo and Janjero, and to the south of Bako and Bulki. This pattern of expansion calls for explanation.

In the area we are considering there are two major language families. Within these families expansion has been explosive. But the two families exist in an envelope composed of two other major language families which have proved church-resistant. The receptive groups are the Ometo group, with Wallamo as its principal member, and the Sidamo group, which includes Kambatta and Darassa. The resistant groups are the Galla and Kaffa families.

The numbers given in tables 1 and 2 represent the percentages of vocabulary shared by the languages listed, and have been compiled by Dr. M. L. Bender through the Language Survey of Ethiopia. Only seven languages from each of the two main groups are listed here, although Dr. Bender's statistics deal with many more.

Table 1 makes it clear that an extensive family exists, reaching from Kullo in the west to Burji in the south, but limited to the

107

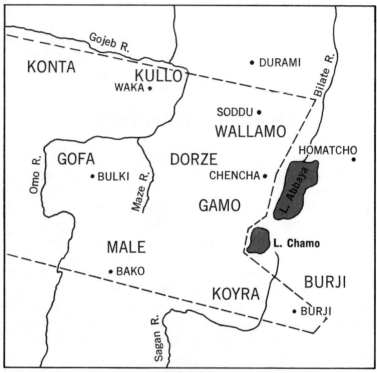

MAP F
THE OMETO LANGUAGE GROUP

TABLE 1
PERCENTAGES OF COMMON VOCABULARY
IN THE OMETO GROUP

	Wallamo	Gamo	Kullo	Dorze	Koyra	Male
Gofa	93	91	84	81	52	46
Wallamo		89	80	80	48	43
Gamo			80	82	49	44
Kullo				73	48	43
Dorze					54	48
Koyra						45

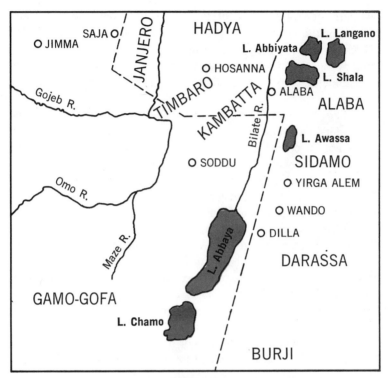

MAP G
THE SIDAMO LANGUAGE GROUP

TABLE 2
PERCENTAGES OF COMMON VOCABULARY
IN THE SIDAMO GROUP

	Kambatta	Timbaro	Alaba	Sidamo	Darassa	Burji
Hadya	61	58	58	58	51	41
Kambatta		86	82	64	54	40
Timbaro			82	64	58	41
Alaba				67	57	42
Sidamo					63	47
Darassa						45

western side of the line of the Bilate river and the two lakes. North of the Gojeb river lie the Kaffa languages; north of Soddu is Kambatta. The area covered by this language family is approximately one hundred twenty-five miles from north to south and the same east to west, a total of some fifteen thousand square miles.

Within this vast crescent Wallamo evangelists could travel and be understood by at least some of the people they encountered. It must not, of course, be supposed that throughout this area all the languages encountered belong to the one family. Particularly to the south the situation is confused linguistically and this situation is reflected in the diminishing percentages of vocabulary agreements between north and south. But it is important that in the area under consideration the languages are related by more than vocabulary: grammar and syntax are also related so that we have to deal with dialects rather than distinct languages.

When we consider the Sidamo group of languages, however, table 2 shows that the percentages of vocabulary agreement are in general lower than for the Ometo group. What is more important is that examination of grammar and syntax of the individual languages shows that they are not mutually intelligible. But still, we again find a great crescent of related languages; Timbaro, Kambatta and Hadya and then Alaba, cut off a little by a range of hills and the Bilate river. Eastward then, into Sidamo, with the Galla languages of Arussi to the north and the Galla tribes of the Bilate lowlands providing a screen from Wallamo westward. And so into Darassa and on south again to Burji.

Although the pioneer SIM party could not have known this when they occupied Kambatta, Wallamo and Sidamo, they were, in fact, staking out an area totaling over twenty-five thousand square miles within which two major language families would facilitate communication. This factor of language must be accounted a major influence in the growth of the church.

The Galla group of languages forms the major part of the envelope within which the church has grown. Northward lies the Arussi desert and the Arussi Galla. To the south, lying between the area under consideration and the Kenya border, are the Borana Galla. Linking the two groups is an attenuated strip of Guji Galla territory, bordering the Bilate river. Eastward are the highland Arussi, on the mountains bordering the Rift Valley, with the Jum-Jum to their south. To the northwest are the Macha Galla.

The Galla invasions of the sixteenth century broke into several streams, pressing up the lowland valleys: the Rift Valley, the valley of the Wabi Shebelli, the Omo Valley. When the pagan Galla came into contact with Christianity it was intimately linked with the Amhara rulers. What is more natural than that the Galla should reject Christianity in favor of Islam, its obvious antithesis? During the seventeenth and eighteenth centuries the Galla empire grew, finally embracing Kambatta and much of Wallamo and bringing the whole into a Galla confederacy. Attempts by Theodore and then by John IV, in the second part of the nineteenth century to bring about a forcible conversion to Christianity failed. It was Menelik II who ended the Galla kingdoms of Kambatta, Wallamo and Kaffa. But although the central core of the area returned almost at once to its fundamentally animistic religion, the region was left with a Moslem mantle, an ethnic discontinuity which proved an effective cultural barrier to the advancing church of Wallamo-Kambatta.

12

1940-1950

In August 1938 the last SIM missionary had left Ethiopia. The great movement of the Spirit was already under way: in the first two years after the departure of the missionaries one hundred and eighty believers were baptized in Koisha alone, and Koisha is merely one of the several districts of Wallamo. Two of the principal evangelists in this area, Toro and Gafato, were imprisoned but, undeterred, Dana Gadaba carried on alone. The two men were sentenced to ten months in prison but on their release the work went on; the number baptized rose to four hundred, then to over a thousand.

Off to the west of Soddu, cut off from the rest of Wallamo by a low range of mountains, lies Fungo. In 1938 Ato Fulasso was sent by the church at Soddu to this remote area; one of the first converts was Ato Kareto, still an elder in the Fungo church thirty years later.

By mid-1939, after three years of occupation, the Italian authorities could still do little more than occupy the principal towns. The wide sweep of the countryside remained the domain of the patriot armies. The Italian governor of Wallamo determined to impress upon the people of his area (which included the whole district to the borders of Lake Chamo) the futility of resistance. He arranged a military parade in Soddu, and sent orders throughout Wallamo and Gamo-Gofa that all men were required to attend the parade. The affair was certainly impressive.

The tribes of the area met together: Wallamo, Gofa, Shankalla, to marvel at the thousands of soldiers and their weapons, the trucks and tanks, the artillery and the rest of Mussolini's war machine. And when the parade was over, the people were left to find

Ethiopian style prayer meeting developed during Italian
occupation

their way home again as best they could. Some of the Gamo people spent the night in Wallamo homes. Four or five found themselves in the home of some Wallamo Christians. As the Christians
told them of their new faith, each of the visitors determined to
accept it too. As best as they could, the Wallamos instructed them
for the rest of the night in the Christian faith. The very next
morning they headed back to Gamo.

The men had come from Ocholo, the prominent mountain peak
near Chencha. Their language is related to Wallamo and there is
an annual link with the Wallamo people who come each year to
work in the lowland cotton fields which stretch between Ocholo
and Lake Abbaya. From these migrant workers the Ocholo people
had heard rumors of the religion which was sweeping Wallamo,
but the movement had not touched them personally. Now the
circle began to widen; one of the four men who went to Soddu
was Ato Gimbo. The first Gamo church was built at Zuza, on
Gimbo's land. Gimbo was a notable first convert, a *halaka,* one
of the ranks of witch doctor, whose principal task is to ensure that
the commands of the qalicha are obeyed. Gimbo set about preaching and the Zuza church community began to grow.

Gimbo was not the only one who came into contact with the Wallamo faith through the parade. Ato Bon'a went, too, and on the way back he heard some children reading a book about God. He could not understand what he heard but he was impressed by it since he was one of those who had forsaken the old Gamo religion under the impetus of the preaching of Ato Esa. This man was one of a trio of prophets who appeared in southern Ethiopia to prepare the way for the evangelists. Esa preached in the nineteen twenties, calling on the Gamo people to abandon the worship of Sala'e, the spirit of evil, to put a stop to the ceremonies at the sacred trees and streams, and to worship God the Creator instead. They were to seek mercy, to offer honey in place of the animal sacrifices and to fast on Fridays. He would place honey on his fingertips and flick it into the sky as an offering to the Creator-God. When Mr. Ohman visited Ocholo in 1933 he was aware of the influence of Esa. People in Ocholo recall how Mr. Ohman took a leaf and tossed it into the sky. As it gently floated back to earth he reminded the people that this was what happened to their offerings of honey: God wanted not their honey, but they themselves.

In Kambatta, at Unfura, the second of the prophets appeared in 1939. Abbaye, a qalicha, suddenly called his neighbors together and told them to stop worshiping Satan: they must believe in Christ. When his astonished listeners asked him who Christ was he told them what he knew, which proved to be little enough. He made them rest on Sundays, and gather to listen to him preach. Among those who heard him was the sister of Abba Gole and she at once recognized that the teaching was that of the "Jesus men," as the believers were called in Kambatta. Ato Moloro also heard the preaching, and went off to Dubancho to bring back Abba Gole. Abba Gole listened, astonished, to the preaching. Turning to the qalicha, whose hair had grown into a matted tangle he said, "What you taught previously was Satan's work. Now teach the truth. Pull down your old house. Build a new one. Have your hair cut off. Drink water; eat your food with gladness."

It remains a mystery where Abbaye received his teaching. He claimed that God spoke to his own heart, directly. When he preached he would hold up the palm of his hand in front of him, and appear to be reading his own palm: "This is what God says."

But he had never seen a Bible and had been a qalicha for as long as he could remember.

The third of the prophets was Chelleke, another qalicha of Gofa. As far back as 1930 he prophesied that men would fly and the mountains shake, prophesies fulfilled when the Italians bombed the district. A later prophecy was more detailed: he would be brought a golden book under the wanza tree by his house, that men with crooked sticks would bring the message by way of the river, that a big house would be built in each village, and that whoever entered the house would save his soul. Then old men would wish they were youths and the youths would wish they were babes.

Chelleke's prophecy was meticulously fulfilled: a Wallamo evangelist made his way up into Gofa, following the course of the river, seeking for Dufarsha, converted through Walter Ohman's preaching before the occupation. But when the evangelist preached, he repeatedly heard the people refer in fear to Chelleke. So he went to see Chelleke. Outside his house, beneath the wanza tree, the evangelist produced a book. Chelleke was only mildly interested—until the book was opened. It was the wordless book. The pages are without writing, but are colored to symbolize the teaching of sin, black; sacrifice, red; salvation, white; and finally, the golden page, for glory. By way of the river, a crooked stick (Wallamo walking sticks are turned over at the top unlike the straight wands of the Gofa people), the wanza tree, a golden book. In many Gofa villages stands the "big house," the Christian church. Esa, Abbaya and Chelleke, formed a strange trio of prophets.

In mid-1940 Gimbo made his way to attend the Wallamo church monthly meeting, and there he met Ato Gofilo and Ato Biramo, who had been sent to the Gamo area by the church at Koysha earlier in the year. Gofilo and Gimbo returned to Gamo together and Gofilo left Gimbo at Ocholo while he pressed on to the Bonke district. He made Kacha his base. Kacha was to prove to be a notable center for advance: churches sprang up all around, at Wasamo, Dolla, Kwili, Seyte, Bul'o, Kuta and Haringa. A man from Banko visited the church at Haringa and when Gofilo visited Banko shortly afterward he found that this man had already gained two more converts. Gofilo took Ato Sheli there to remain as evangelist in the Banko area. Gofilo's own work up in the Chencha area was cut short after only a year when he was imprisoned, but already the foundations had been laid.

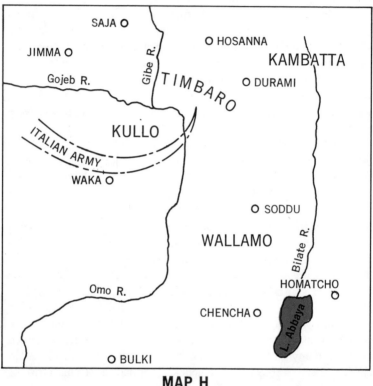

MAP H
THE ITALIAN ARMY OPERATION IN KULLO

In 1939 the Italian parade at Soddu opened the way into Ocholo and the mountains of Chencha. In 1940 an army sweep through Kullo sent the movement westward. The Omo river forms a natural barrier between Wallamo and Kullo, the Gojeb river encircling Kullo country to the north and cutting it off from Jimma. See map H. During the years of the occupation, patriot activity in Kaffa province was widespread. Dejazmatch Arega led an army in the Garada district and Adeno Bora had a large following in Konta. The Italian forces concentrated at Jimma and Waka.

They determined on a sweep through Kullo country, in a scythe-like movement intended to gather up the patriot forces and drive them into the arms of waiting Italian forces in Timbaro. The operation was not a success. Inevitably the patriot armies simply infiltrated behind the Italian lines at night, while the ordinary people were trapped in the net and whole villages were dislocated. Thousands of Kullo people were forced across the Omo river into Timbaro, just east of the confluence of the Gojeb and Omo rivers.

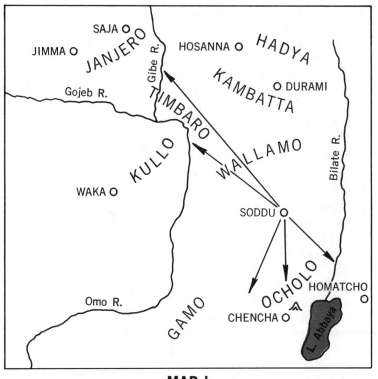

MAP I
EXPANSION FROM WALLAMO

Timbaro forms part of the Kambatta area and SIM missionaries had preached there several years before, but without success. When the Wallamo church heard of the arrival of the Kullo refugees, they at once sent Ato Umboli and Ato Godana Gutullo as evangelists.

One of their first converts was a Timbaro man, Ato Aldada, who has for many years led the Kullo church, although he is not a Kullo himself.

The Wallamo church was not only reaching out to new areas: within Wallamo itself the church was growing fast. See map I. In 1943 Wallamo was visited by Guy Playfair, the SIM's second general director. At his suggestion the Wallamo district was divided into three areas and the number of main elders was increased to fifteen. Two years later the Ohmans, Miss Bergsten and Miss Barnard, a nurse, returned to Soddu. They settled in the town. Temporarily they were refused permission to visit the churches and so the Christians came to them. In October they had twelve hundred visitors, in December the register records seven women's meetings, nine men's classes, ninety-two services and almost fifteen hundred visitors. By January 1946 visitors passed the two thousand mark, but at last, on November 2 the missionaries were able to go back to the old Otona site. The Emperor had hoped that a government-operated hospital might be built there, but when this proved impossible the mission was asked to operate a hospital for the area. Dr. Barlow was the first SIM doctor in the hospital up on Otona hill after the Italian days. The place was a shambles: it had been used by the Italians as an army camp; following their defeat it became their prison. For several years it had been derelict. The stone buildings were quickly cleaned up and mission work began again.

The growth continued: in 1946 the system of districts was again expanded to form eight districts. In April 1947 a Bible school opened and by August there were 97 enrolled. In November came the first Wallamo Conference with Mr. and Mrs. Playfair and C. Gordon Beacham among the visitors. At a local baptismal service ninety-nine were baptized. Out in the churches Miss Bergsten was conducting women's classes and in 1948 Ruth Martin followed her example and conducted a series of teacher training courses all over Wallamo.

The work to the south and west was going ahead, too. Up in Gamo churches were being planted; in 1948 Glen Cain, who had been in the army up to this point, returned to Ethiopia as the field director and took Walter Ohman with him on a trip to Chencha to see at first hand what was going on. It was obvious that the mission would soon have a part to play in the work: in November 1949 Mr. and Mrs. Ed Ratzliff had started building there. Already there were five churches, at Zuza, at Digido, in Boroda, and two in Dudene.

With the departure of the Italians, the Kullo Christians who had remained, occupying the eastern bank of the Omo, in Timbaro, were free to return home. By 1947 they were mostly back across the river. The first four Kullo churches lie in a line on the southern bank of the Omo. They took evangelists back with them, too: Ato Umboli, Ato Maja Madero and Ato Madalcho Gessame, all of whom had been neighbors back at Obicho in Wallamo, and, of course, Aldada. Here, too, the churches flourished: four in 1947, eight by 1950, seven were begun by refugees from Timbaro, the eighth was started at Buri by refugees who had crossed the Omo further south into Wallamo country.

The Kullo officials were suspicious of the new movement. The leaders were arrested and imprisoned. Ato Hatassa picked up a disease in the prison and, although he was released, he died at home shortly afterwards. Ato Dubba and Ato Kurra, two more Wallamo evangelists, accompanied by a young lad, came into Kullo and all three were arrested. The lad died. When the two men were released after a year they were ordered back to Wallamo. When the other men were freed they were forbidden to preach until they could produce an official permit from the capital.

The decade was to see further advances from Wallamo yet. Beyond the Gojeb River and to the west of the Omo lies Janjero. In April 1948 Mr. Healy and George Leighton pitched their tent under the huge fig tree which is still the prominent feature of the Saja mission station. In Addis Ababa the mission opened a secondary school, the Christian Training Institute, with Rev. Mel Holsteen as director.[1] Two of the older students, Lij Kassa and Ishetu, were sent down to Saja to help in the work. Lij Kassa went out visiting, trekking, and preaching up in Janjero country. A few responded, among them two young men, Habte-Maryam and Haile-Maryam. A few days before the CTI students were to return to school, they took these two converts and a record player and

1. The school later became the Girls' Christian Academy. Lij Kassa was appointed the administrator while his wife, Esther, taught for many years in the school.

trekked up to Saturday market. The warm reception given to them by the local people raised the bitter antagonism of the local school headmaster. On their way back to Saja the little party was set upon by a mob of school children. The group finally reached Saja, their clothes having been torn and their food stolen. Somewhat discouraged, Ishetu and Lij Kassa returned to Addis Ababa.

But the nucleus of believers was growing: Tekle-Mangasha and Zeggeye were converted down at Saja through the preaching of the missionaries and started a church at Gannita. News of the little group reached Wallamo and, ever on the alert for new ways of spreading the fire, the Wallamo church sent in Ato Shunke and Ato Elyas to help the Janjero work. Basing themselves at Tekle-Mangasha's house they began to preach through the area. North, south, west and even to the east the work was growing.

In 1950 there were some two hundred churches in Wallamo, five up in the Chencha area, two more in Bulki, eight across in Kullo country and just one in Janjero. In one way or another all traced their origins to the pioneer party that had camped on the spine of the hill jutting out from Mount Damota at Otona.

In Kambatta Clarence Duff believes that the presence of the missionaries had been a positive hindrance once the first converts had been made. The rest of the people were convinced that the new faith of Shigute and Sabaro and Shibashi was simply a prudent insurance policy for their jobs with the missionaries. When the missionaries left, it was confidently expected that the men would at once return to their old ways. When they didn't, interest was stirred up. The church began to grow: first came Dubancho and then Ambursi, home of Abba Gole. The first church in the Durami area came from Abba Gole's preaching at Mishgida. Then Benara, and Zato, on land belonging to Ato Bachore. Bachore's brother was a qalicha: when Bachore refused to let his brother take his children to assist in his practices, a curse was placed on them. Four of them died.

But his wife's sister was a believer. Her husband, also was a believer (and later their son, Dr. Mulatu, was administrator of the SIM's leprosarium at Shashamane) and the couple went to Bachore to assure him that the qalicha's power could be broken if he became a Christian. It took his own illness to drive him to take this step. When he recovered, his first action was to have a church built on his land at Zato.

In 1946 there were a hundred churches in Kambatta. Dr. Wilson and Alf Roke, another of the pre-occupation missionaries to return, began to truck in supplies for the reopening of the work at Hosanna. On July 13, 1946 Dr. and Mrs. Wilson and Miss Warhanik reached Dubancho. On their first Sunday three hundred and fifty gathered for the service. The following November the missionaries watched as 104 Kambattans were baptized. And in February the elders reported to Dr. Wilson that there were now 110 churches in Kambatta-Gudeila, and another five on the west side of the Omo River comprised of former Timbaro refugees.

The churches continued to reach out: Abba Gole spent most of his days touring Kambatta, his parish. Untiringly he preached. By the end of the ten years there were 145 churches in Kambatta.

Then there was Sidamo. When the missionaries returned there in 1946 they found that the few believers they had left behind had been almost wiped out by a typhoid epidemic in 1940. Only Ato Werrera and Ato Ganame were left of the original group. Alf Roke moved into Homatcho in 1946, joined in May by Mr. and Mrs. Delmer Stevens. Mr. Stevens was an indefatigable trekker and he quartered methodically over Sidamo, especially out in the Yenasse district. In September 1947 Homatcho was exchanged as a mission station for Wando and in August 1949 the first Sidamo church was opened at Homatcho. The Wallamos sent Ato Shanka across to help. When he arrived he found that there were already ten converts at Hida, a little to the north. Then came Anole, opened in October 1949 and only a month later there were seventy present at a fellowship meeting at Hida. This was followed in spite of mounting opposition in July 1950 by the first baptismal service since the return of the missionaries. Another sixty-six were baptized at Gunde in September. There are four churches now.

Acting as a buffer for the three principal areas, Kambatta, Wallamo and Sidamo is Shashamane, with the predominately Moslem Arussi Galla to the north of the town. See map J. The land in the immediate vicinity of Shashamane is very fertile, and both Kambattan and Wallamo settlers are sprinkled liberally throughout the area. These settlers take a calculated risk, for the

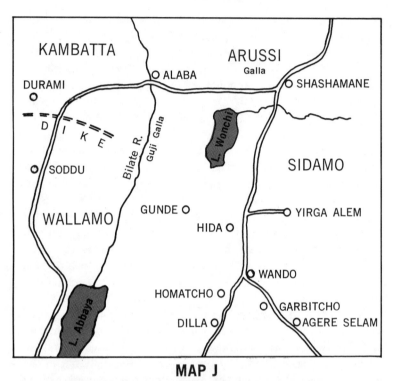

MAP J
SHASHAMANE: WHERE FOUR TRIBES MEET

Arussi have not forgotten that they once held land far into what is now Wallamo territory. Somewhere around the beginning of the present century the Wallamos expelled them from the land south of Alaba and constructed a tremendous dike and wall to mark the boundary. Sections of the dike and wall can still be seen north of Soddu and as far west as the Omo valley. But already the Wallamo boundary is far beyond the dike.

When Laurie Davison was in Wallamo shortly after his return, he called Ato Cheramo to the Shashamane area to evangelize. Although Cheramo did not stay long, he was followed by other Wallamo evangelists including Ato Galore. Kambattan evangelists followed their example. The first church was at Goba (not to be confused with Goba in Bale province) when a Wallamo farmer crossed the Bilate River valley and then invited a Wallamo evangelist to use his home as a base for evangelizing the district. This proved to be fairly typical of church development in this area: more than half the churches in the Shashamane area owe their origins to Kambattan or Wallamo settlers.

Out in the Siraro area, where Cliff Mitchell and Tom Devers lost their lives, one group of Kambattans and another of Wallamos settled. When Rev. Tommy Simpson and Mr. Alan Neal went out to visit them they found that there had been thirteen conversions through the Wallamo group and thirty-three through the Kambattans (Did language make this much difference? Or did the lingering memory of defeat keep the Arussi away from the Wallamos?)

The Brants had opened the work in Shashamane for the SIM in April 1947 and developed a pattern of outreach which was to prove most effective further south. Mrs. Brant opened a clinic while her husband spent his time traveling and preaching. After only a year the Brants headed for Dilla, some twenty-five miles south of Wando. The lowland plains were largely uninhabited then, and Mr. Brant spent days toiling up the mountains to the east, preaching to the Darassa people. The work was hard and still in 1950 there was but little evidence of the scores of churches one day to be scattered throughout the Darassa district.

Strangely, already the sense of awe was beginning to pass from the missionaries. New workers were coming out who had not seen the early barren years. They took for granted the churches, the scurrying figures of the evangelists, the overwhelming baptismal services. Only the veterans: the Ohmans, the Cains, Miss Bergsten, Mr. Roke, could really measure the magnitude of a miracle: more than three hundred and fifty churches, packed every Sunday in what once was pagan southern Ethiopia.

13

The Gods of the South

One of the immediate results of the great movement in southern Ethiopia was the liberation of the believers from their fear of the spirits. Ato Shigute, in Kambatta illustrates the transformation perfectly. He and his brother bought a goat at the market and slaughtered it. In the traditional manner his brother cut off a portion of the meat and placed it at the foot of a sacred tree as an offering to Satan. Shigute promptly went forward and recovered half of the chunk of meat. "Don't give it away. Satan has no power," he asserted. "He can't eat. I don't mean to waste my money; I shall take my share of the meat. Of course, you can do as you wish with yours. I mean to eat mine: there's nothing to fear."

The two brothers stood arguing about the fearsomeness of Satan. Just then a neighbor of theirs, Haile-Maryam, came along. Having seen what happened, he concluded that if Shigute didn't die within the day, then he should believe in Christ too. He watched Shigute eat his meat, and then for a couple of days he followed him around. Nothing happened. Haile-Maryam began to tell everybody what Shigute had done, and he himself became a believer.

The old religion was called *Fandancho,* and offerings were made to Magano, perhaps in thanks for healing, for some miraculous intervention or to invoke his aid. The offerings were made sometimes to the sacred trees, more often to the *Tankway*[1] who also laid claim to the clothing of the dead. There was also a distinct hierarchy of Tankway, who claimed to be manifestations of Magano, and called *Kilancho.* Up on Ambaricho Mountain which

1. From the Amharic verb *Teneqola,* meaning the practice of the occult.

looms over the Durami mission station was one such man, a famed rainmaker. At Mishgida was Ato Fota, who was called in by childless women, or by women whose children were sick. At Kacha was Ato Ingilala, the god of the warriors.

The generally animistic worship of the area, however, centered on sacred trees and groves. The Fandancho was principally an individualistic religion, not a communal one. True, there was the annual fifteen day fast, possibly copied from the Moslems, for Mohammed Grany had established a shortlived Moslem state in Kambatta in the sixteenth century, but the fast was only observed sporadically. In theory no food was to be taken between sunrise and sunset, but few went to such lengths.

Some customs could be adapted to form a basis for Bible instruction, particularly Old Testament practices. Across in Sidamo, sacrifices were made on a hill, set aside by the tribe as its sacred hill. Such hills can be seen in many parts of Sidamo, Arussi and Gamo-Gofa, often crowned with trees, while all the neighboring hills are stripped of all greenery. The trees on a sacred hill are tabu. On the sacred hill the sacrifice was killed, the hide of the animal carefully divided and the entire carcase similarly equally divided and laid on the two halves of the skin. Some of the blood was taken on the fingertips and flicked skyward with the invocation "May it reach you" (rather as the prophet Esa had done with honey in Chencha). Various crops were added to the carcass, together with salt, and the whole was consumed in a blazing pyre.

The principle of making offerings to God was well-established: everywhere in the south the first few drops of coffee are spilt onto the ground as an offering to the spirits and even Orthodox Christians observe this obviously pagan custom. The annual sacrifice, however, was aimed at gaining freedom from the power of the spirits. After being sprinkled with blood from the sacrifice, the entire clan would pass through low archways constructed from the branches of shrubs and trees, in symbol leaving the spirits on the wrong side of the archways. The Wallamo people believed firmly that each man is followed by an *uqabe,* an evil spirit, who is responsible for all his troubles. Even today it is unnerving to be driving in Wallamo and have someone dart out from the bush at the side of the track and rush across in front of the truck, in the hope of cutting off the uqabe.

Further down the Rift Valley are the Darassa people. Their god, evidently related to the god of the Kambattans, is Magana, the creator, but their worship centers on Durissa,[2] whom the Christians identify with Satan. They divide Darassa country into seven districts, each with its own *tolcha sango,* or place of sacrifice. The elders of each area decide among themselves when, for their own area, the tolcha should be offered. The time may be influenced by some tribal misfortune, but in any event the tolcha may be offered only once each year. It normally consists of a sheep. The animal is taken, one eye is put out, one leg broken, one ear cut off and then the sacrifice is thrown onto a pyre to be consumed. Here again the intention of the sacrifice is to obtain respite for the tribe from the attentions of Durissa.

From Bulki, in Gofa district, the story of Mitsa Shara reveals the same fear of the spirits. This man's father was plowing when he suddenly screamed with a mixture of pain and fear: Satan had struck him with something white out of the ground, and his arm was broken. The family took this to mean that Satan had claimed the land for himself and they were no longer allowed to plow it. And then the endless round of visits to the witch doctors, qalichas, began. They demanded sacrifices: a red hen and a black sheep daily, and a white cow to be sacrificed at the spot where the accident happened. A red cow was slaughtered and its blood collected in a wooden basin. Rancid butter and a large quantity of honey were heated and mixed with the blood. The fire used to heat this concoction had to be made from twelve different varieties of wood. The victim was to take two cupfuls of the mixture each morning. On the first morning he managed to get one cupful down, but the second made him vomit. Mitsa Shara begged his father to let him take him down to the Christians at Goybe, but he refused. Unable to take the qalicha's medicine, he eventually died.

With others of the family also ill, Mitsa Shara was at his wits end. He sacrificed a goat and examined the entrails for a sign

2. When I asked people why they worshiped Durissa and not Magana, they replied that Magana was remote, in no way involved in this world beyond the act of creation. It was the revelation that this far off Creator-God was, in fact, a God-at-hand which so attracted the Darassa people. This is particularly interesting when taken with Stephen Neill's comments on the knowledge of a high God filtering down into Buganda from Ethiopia. See Stephen Neill's *Christian Faith and Other Faiths,* pp. 143-46.

regarding the outcome of the illness of his children, but seemed to get no answer. So, summoning up all his courage, he went to visit the Christians. Assured of their power, he went that following Sunday to their church and accepted Christ. Returning home he threw out of the house all the objects connected with the old religion. Another decisive break with the old, and a remarkable boldness in making the new faith work.

The old Gofa religion had one man as its leader, called Kawa Toga. *Kawa,* like *Kowna* in Wallamo, means chief. He is the rain-maker, the one who causes crops to grow, the one who guaran-tees the fertility of the women. The people believe that the god who created heaven and earth lives in the water. Kawa Toga leads the people to the river, and there a cow is sacrificed. Then he plunges his hand into the water and what he brings out is an omen of what the coming year holds. Grain in the hand means a good harvest. An empty hand means famine.

Describing the traditional beliefs of the country, one man told me:

> This is the manner of placating god in my country. The god who made heaven and earth lives in the water. People from the whole district bring money and give it to the lake. They bring it from all the six *balabbat* disrticts.[3] Men are chosen to take the gifts into the water, which is on top of a great mountain. They prepare *shammas* (the white shawl which is worn by both men and women, draped around the shoulders), iron rods, a black sheep and a black goat, a black cow and grain. The seven men take the gifts. Four rivers flow from the lake in which the woman lives in a house (the creator-god is a woman). Even today people believe in her. The men take the gifts into the water by a marked path. At the house there are guardians: a lion, a snake and a man, but they must pass through the midst of them. They spend seven days there (note that the house is supposed to be under the lake, not on an island).[4] When they come out of the water, four of the men are killed and the re-maining three return to their homes.
>
> Because these gifts have been given, it is expected that chil-

3. A *balabbat* is a minor official, a district governor, but more a land-lord than a civil servant.
4. See Malcolm Forsberg's *Land Beyond the Nile*, p. 154. A Maban witch doctor was reported to have hidden from his pursuers for three days by sitting beneath the water of a stream.

Man wearing *shamma*

dren will grow very tall, and because of the iron rods people will be strong and not die. This is sufficient for seven years, but for many years there has been no offering and this is blamed by the people for the short children and the many deaths in the district. This I have not seen for myself, but my father told me about it. The mountain is called Zam, and it is in the Zift district. The main river is called Irgina. The name of the creator is Indak.

There is a variety of gradations in the hierarchy of the Tankways, one of the most interesting being the *Mero,* or stone counter. He is subordinate to the Tankway but may graduate to the higher position. Near Chencha in Gamo district, among the Ocholo people, the Mero uses either twenty-nine or thirty-two stones. The pile of stones is first divided arbitrarily into two piles, one of which is temporarily discarded. The remaining pile is systematically reduced, two by two, until eventually the Mero is left either with one stone or two. These are then placed by themselves. The whole collection of stones, except for the one or two which formed the remnant, is brought together and again arbitrarily divided. Again one pile is discarded and the second pile reduced two by two until only one stone or two are left. This remainder is placed next to, but separate from the first remnant. The counting process reading of the future of the person on whose behalf the stones emerges, each spot occupied by either a single stone or by two stones. The final pattern of stones then determines the Mero's reading of the future of the person on whose behalf the stones are being consulted.

Ato Jubato, who described all this, was himself a Mero before his conversion. He consulted his stones when one of his children was taken ill. As the pattern was completed he saw that the two spots at the head of the columns were occupied by two stones each. This indicated death. Hoping to escape from the power of the stones he took his child away from the house and placed her in the shelter of a huge rock. But on the third day she died. Jubato went home in despair and threw his stones away, but his terrified neighbors flocked into the house, begging him to restore them: he had to place them on his bed, anoint them with butter and cover them with his shamma. The deaths of three of his children were predicted in the same implacable manner: eventually

Jubato determined to seek out the new religion which he had heard had entered Ocholo. But as he was leaving his house to go to the church at Zuza, he met Ato Boka, who had come to speak to him about Christ. Jubato became a Christian and Boka was sent by the church to become the evangelist in Jubato's district.

Circumcision is practiced throughout Ethiopia, but is usually effected in infancy or at puberty. Among the Galla tribes there is no fixed age for circumcision since circumcision is tied to the *gada* system of age-sets. Among the Galeb, the people of the area around Bako, however, men are not circumcised until they reach the age when they may take wives. A man is permitted to have up to five wives. All the young men assemble at one place and a round hole is bored in the ground and the men then sit around with their knives. At a signal given by the oldest man in the district, each circumcises himself, the blood draining into the hole. After this the hole is closed and the men go back to a new hut, especially built for them. The men who are circumcised on the same day then become a single tribal unit.

Ato Birhanu Getahun, who was formerly health officer in the Bako district, recorded the traditional account of the origins of Bako, Male and Banna tribes:

> Long ago three brothers, named Bako, Male and Banna, came from a faraway place which no one can tell up to now, and were found in a tree by a chieftain of the place, who was out hunting. When he saw them he ordered his followers to get hold of them, and to put them in a place from which they could not escape. The order was followed, and they were kept in a little hut adjacent to the living quarters of the chief. They were left there for over a week, fed very well, and cared for as if they were the children of the chief. All this was done to test the brothers. But in the second week the chief called all his subordinates to a gathering and told them he wanted to adopt these three wanderers as his children, for he had none. All the people agreed to his suggestion, and the three brothers were set free to enjoy the freedom that the children of the big chief, like the one who arrested them, would enjoy. They later on married the daughters of the other chiefs of the area.
>
> After a long stay with these people, the three brothers decided to leave the area. But one of them brought the idea that they were brought up in such an aristocratic manner that it

would be shameful, as well as unwise, to leave the chief, who was growing old, without any support. Another idea was brought by one of them; the idea was to cast lots, and the one whose fate it was to stay behind should help the old chief and inherit his position. They agreed, and lots were cast and the chance fell on Male.

Now the other two were left to decide which way to go. They finally chose two hills: Bako moved to the hill in the north, Banna decided to move to the hill in the south with his family. The hill he chose is called *Zequala*.[5] This was so arranged to have Male between their tribes. Later on, as generation followed generation they intermarried. But the Male and Banna tribes later quarrelled, although the Bako tribe remained as friendly as ever with both tribes.

The status of a man at his death is determined by his life history. In the Wallamo group, circumcision determines the manner of burial. In general, burial takes place on the day of the death, even if death takes place late in the evening. In most parts of the country there are *mahabir* fellowships, and each member of a mahabir is expected to attend the funeral of another member. Extravagant signs of mourning, even to the extent of the gashing of the face and breast are expected at the *likso* or funeral. Even the word itself is indicative of the attitude toward death. *Likso* comes from the Amharic word *alakkasa* "to weep." Ritual dances are frequent. In Wallamo the chief mourners throw themselves to the ground, and may have to be supported as the dance is prolonged.

Some of the customs mentioned above are exemplified by tribes in the Bako area, where the contrasting custom of mummification of a dead chief is practiced. Among the Bako tribe, for example, if a chief dies, a particular clan, familiar with funeral rites, is summoned, and they prepare the body for burial. At the funeral gathering the nearest relative of the deceased stands in the middle of the crowd of mourners. By his side a young man takes his place, carrying spear and shield. A man wishing to express his grief rushes out, shaking his spear and shouting the praises of the dead man. He then strikes the shield with his spear. Failure to

5. Not to be confused with the Mount Zuquala to the south of Addis Ababa, the extinct volcano, site of a church and goal of pilgrimage for Orthodox Christians.

pierce the shield is a terrible shame: such a man would find it next to impossible to obtain a wife.

Among the Male the death of an ordinary member of the tribe is followed by a likso where the relatives sing funeral songs. The men leap into the air and fall flat onto the ground, apparently in an attempt to attract the attention of the spirits and to show their grief so that the spirits might take pity on them. The body is tied with the knees flexed to the chest. As among the Wallamos the grave is first dug vertically and then a further sideways recess prepared into which the body is placed. Finally an ox is killed and feasted on before the burial place is left.

If the dead man was a chief, his best ox is killed and his body is wrapped in the ox skin and kept in a newly built hut. It is left there for a year with a fire burning continuously by the side of the corpse. The body is cared for by a clan specializing in this duty. During the year the chief is not counted as dead, but at some time in the year a successor to the dead man is chosen. When a year has elapsed the dead chief is buried in the same manner as any ordinary member of the tribe. Whether the dead man was a chief or not, all his possessions are destroyed after the funeral.

Among the Hamer and Galeb tribes a similar process of mummification of a chief is observed. The hands of the corpse are left protruding from the ox skin and the people may then bring to him whatever they think he may need. For at least six months the body is kept in this manner and then the chief's death is announced. The skin is slit open, the body tied with flexed knees and placed in a sitting position in a vertical, cylindrical shaft. An ordinary man is buried in the same way on the day of his death. Burial is the task of the women. An exception is made for a man killed in battle. Then his body is not buried, but left on the battlefield for the vultures to feed on. No mourning is allowed in such a case. On the contrary there is tribal singing and dancing, tokens of the death of a hero. The death customs of the Mursi follow the same general pattern.

The Chabo Galla, situated southwest of Addis Ababa and to the immediate north of the Kambatta district present an interesting contrast since they mix the customs typical of much of the rest of the south, the observation of fasts, the offering of coffee to the spirits, with a semi-matriarchal *Atete*-cult.[6] Atete is the female deity and Astaro the subordinate male deity. On the day known as *Astaro-Maryam,* grain is taken by the women up to the hill-tops to be offered to Astaro. Immediately after this there will be a meeting of the Orthodox Mary-mahabir in a curious blend of the pagan and the Christian.

For the female deity each family chooses a cow, which is then called the Atete cow; everything connected with it, even to its dung, is then counted sacred. When the family holds an Atete feast, butter is made from the cow's milk and each member of the household is anointed on the head and on the base of the neck. The milk is consecrated by one of the elders present, who spits into it, and the milk is then drunk by the family. Spitting is a common feature of many consecration rites of the Galla.

The secrets of the *moyat,* an association of women for religious purposes, are carefully preserved; initiation usually takes place before a girl is married and it is practically impossible for her to leave the moyat afterward. The initiation ceremony includes the eating of a narcotic root. The women who lead the moyat call the devotees together by wild running and crying while they wave two branches in front of them. All members then have to drop what they are doing to attend the moyat. In the days following the open-ing of the SIM mission work at Wolisso these women were fre-quently seen circling the mission station, but the practice is no longer as common as it once was.

In examining the religion of the people of the south it is at once apparent that the church has grown up almost exclusively in a pagan society, the mainly Moslem Galla peoples proving resistant to the advancing church. A plurality of gods, a multiplicity of spirits, a fear of inexplicable tabus, a fear of gods untouched by any feeling of pity has been replaced by a vigorous dependence on Christ. For the Christian, old things have passed away, every-thing has become new.

6. See Alan R. Tippett, *Peoples of Southwest Ethiopia,* p. 157. The Maram cult referred to by Tippett is the Mary-mahabir of the Orthodox church.

14

1950-1960

Opposition to the church in Kambatta appeared to grow in the same proportion as the church grew. In April 1947 thirty new believers were imprisoned, and throughout 1947 and into 1948 the persecution continued unabated. In 1949 the Kambatta church decided that action must be taken to protect the church and sent Ato Ababa Bushiro to the capital with a letter to the Emperor. There is a traditional way of delivering such a letter and Ababa was the man to make use of it. When the Emperor was out in his car somewhere near the great shola tree on the road to the north, Ababa flung himself to the ground in front of the wheels of the Rolls-Royce. When the car stopped, the Emperor asked if Ababa's *abeituta* or plea, was oral or written. Ababa produced the letter which the Emperor accepted. In due course, the Emperor ordered the governor-general of Shoa province, H. E. Asrate Kassa,[1] to investigate the accusations. The outcome of these investigations belongs to the next chapter, but they were in the main helpful to the suffering church. Less helpful, however, was the trouble that now burst on the believers.

Education was the difficulty. Three elders, recognizing their lack of education, asked for permission to go to school. The rest of the elders procrastinated and gave no answer. Instead, they began ignoring the three men. They stopped visiting one another. Charge and counter-charge was raised until the church split. Seventeen churches followed the three, the other hundred and twenty-eight remained with the main fellowship. The missionaries found them-

1. He received theological training at the evangelical Bible Training Institute, Glasgow.

selves unable to advise the church: Norman Couser at Hosanna was both a missionary and an elder of the church.[2]

Fortunately Guy Playfair, the SIM general director, had been invited to speak at the Kambatta annual conference. In 1951 the conference took place at Hosanna in the most unpromising of circumstances. But one sermon brought the entire conference to a standstill. Guy Playfair spoke of a corn of wheat, sown to produce perhaps fifty seeds. These are sown again to produce two thousand more, and in turn these produced one hundred thousand. The Kambattan people could see the fields of grain, ripening in the warm sun; all from one seed. Then Playfair asked: "Who will be that seed?" From everywhere men began to stand up, and women too, offering to support the evangelists. The program came to a halt and late into the night the counselling went on, men being attracted in from the nearby trails to see this strange moving of God in Kambatta. More than one hundred and forty men finally offered themselves as evangelists.

Meanwhile there was the other matter to be settled. Miss Macomber was brought in as interpreter. For two days the hearing went on. The three elders complained of the procrastination of the rest in replying to their request, accusing the four senior elders of taking too much authority upon themselves. Playfair listened to it all; and, as it was time for him to leave for Wallamo, he promised that he would send them his decision after he had prayed about the matter. Eventually his written judgment arrived. He had decided that:

1. The splinter group was wrong in separating from the rest.
2. The main elders were at fault in delaying for five years in dealing with the request of the three for education.
3. Some accusations, brought against various elders in the past had been misjudged and must be reheard.

2. David Barrett's appreciation of the situation in southern Ethiopia as presented in his book, *Schism and Renewal in Africa,* is in error in a number of respects. There was no time when the church refused to accept mission discipline, because the mission was never in a position to administer discipline (pp. 31, 55, 183).

The breakaway group *may* be termed "the drinking group" by some uncharitable missionaries, but careful study of the events makes clear that this was not the major issue. It would be grossly unfair to the *Makane-Yesus* churches (breakaway group) to suggest that they encourage drinking. The use of intoxicating liquor is not a matter for church discipline among them (p. 291).

4. The ban on greeting one another, on visiting in the home and on using one another's schools was wrong. The main elders had already acknowledged their error in this; now the splinter group were at fault in their spirit of bitterness over the matter.

5. The splinter group should now return to the main fellowship. Such individuals as had been disciplined must, however, complete their period of discipline before being received back into the church.

6. A new constitution should be worked out to ensure that such confusion did not arise again.[3]

In Kambatta there were now 145 churches and, according to a letter from Rev. Melvin Donald to the SIM administration, there were some thirty-three thousand believers. Some of them were already being employed as evangelists by the Norwegian Lutheran Mission, across in Sidamo.

The Lutherans had arrived in Dilla within hours of the arrival of the Brants of the SIM. For the first three years the work was slow, but in 1951 there came a quickening of the pace. In the NLM's year book for 1951, Mr. Gudmund Vinskei wrote: "At the end of last year we had only two congregations, but this year, progress is wonderful."

By 1960 the Lutherans had thirty-nine congregations in Ethiopia, most of them in the Sidamo area. Since the Sidamo language is related to the Kambatta language it was only sense to use Kambattan evangelists for the new outreach. A number of these men started work with the Norwegians, on an informal basis, while the two missions tried to reach agreement on principles of cooperation.

An immediate problem was the salary paid by the NLM to the evangelists. The SIM never paid evangelists, and where evangelists were sent out by the church they were supported by the church. Mr. Cain, the SIM's field director, advised that if evangelists were sent to work with the NLM they must be sent by and supported by the church. Second, they must be free to teach those doctrines which they themselves had accepted in Kambatta. Third, those evangelists already unofficially at work in Sidamo must return to Kambatta to regularize the position with the churches there.

3. Ato Emmanuel Gabre-Sellassie, then on the staff of the British Embassy and now with Radio Voice of the Gospel, went to Kambatta to assist in framing the new constitution.

Mr. Mageroy and Mr. Vinskei of the NLM traveled across to Kambatta to meet with Mr. Donald in the hope of receiving some help for the work in Sidamo. Predictably the two groups failed to reach any agreement. Mr. Cain was clearly right: to have two groups of men going out from one church but supported at different rates could only bring discord. But Mr. Donald's helplessness was the more poignant since only shortly after this meeting he had informed Mr. Cain that of the 140 men who had offered themselves as evangelists the previous year, only some dozen were in fact out preaching. The churches could not properly support them. And yet here were the Lutherans ready to put them to work. Some few of the Kambattans across in Sidamo returned to their churches in Kambatta, most simply got on with their work. And as the Sidamo churches grew, the need for the Kambattans diminished.

Guy Playfair's experiences in Kambatta were duplicated at the Wallamo conference when one hundred and ten men offered themselves as evangelists. They were needed. Down at Burji, Alex Fellows had opened SIM work in as isolated a location as could be found in the south. The work was slow, with perhaps ten converts that first year, 1950. But Mr. Fellows sent to Wallamo for help and Ato Ganebo and Ato Kusa came to Burji.

The two men returned to Wallamo, and Kusa remained there, but soon Ganebo was back, bringing with him Ato Maja, Ato Mune and Ato Andreas. On March 1, 1953 Dana Maja, leader of the Wallamo church, and Ato Tantu came to Burji to examine the first candidates for baptism and to conduct the baptismal service. Twelve men were approved: Masha Bori and his son Boko, Challi, Mamo, Irbo, Bogalla, Guyo, Sheggadi, Sodi, Aimi, Jarso and Gazzu. Ato Giyorgis, from the Chencha area, about halfway between Wallamo and Burji, had led the two Wallamo elders to Burji. Now Mr. Fellows invited him to come to Burji as an evangelist. On his way back to Chencha to obtain permission from the church elders, Giyorgis paused at the village of Manana and spoke with Ato Buja. Buja professed to be converted. Leaving a booklet with him, Giyorgis pressed on to Chencha, promising to return. By the time he reached Manana again, Buja had already produced ten more converts. Among the ten was Ato Taddese, who had suffered for two years from an internal hemorrhage. His bleeding stopped: as a consequence many of the Manana people became Christians.

The Manana church had an eventful history, being burned down in its first year during a bout of opposition. The new building was similarly burned down. But the church continued to grow: Maze and Gacho churches owe their origins to Manana and so rapidly did the work go ahead that Giyorgis had to send for help to Burji: Ato Maja was allocated to Maze church, Ato Matewos to Gacho church and Ato Anjulo assisted Giyorgis at Manana.

The great Wallamo conference in 1951 had been attended by Umboli, Madalcho and Aldada from Kullo, across the Omo river. They asked Mr. Ohman for SIM help in Kullo country. When they returned to their churches they took Mr. and Mrs. Ohman and Dr. Wilson with them to open negotiations for a mission station. The manner in which the required negotiations were completed is interesting. While the Wallamo evangelists had been in prison in Kullo, food was brought to them by a Kullo convert, Tona Jaggo. He was related to a local chief, Danya Dale Daimo. Dale had acted as *wass,* or guarantor, for the evangelists when the judge offered to release them. Now it was suggested that the missionaries should approach Danya Dale to see if he could help again. He was most cooperative. A site was selected, a provisional contract signed and, much sooner than they had anticipated, the missionaries were able to leave. Dr. Wilson returned to Jimma to contact Bob King about entering the new work and the Ohmans headed back to Wallamo. Emulating the wise men, they returned another way. On their journey to Waka they had found the Omo too deep to ford and had been obliged to build a raft on which to make a precarious crossing.

In June 1952 Mr. Ohman made the trip in from Jimma, accompanied by Mr. King, to finalize the land agreement. Remembering his previous experience, Mr. Ohman took along an inflatable raft for the crossing of the Gojeb river. By the end of July all was ready for occupying Waka and then the rains came. Bob King went off to help with the building work at Agaro until the rains lifted. Finally, on November 13, with twenty-three mules and numerous carriers, he set off for Waka. The first day brought trouble: a hyena attacked and killed one of the animals. The guides quarrelled. The caravan split. As the journey progressed, troubles multiplied: mules fell over the cliffs. One was discovered on a ledge, stranded on its back with its pack still intact. And

Single-engine MAF plane

even when they reached Waka there was a hostile reception. Not for three years would there be a church in the Waka district, although further north there were already eight.

The qalichas were called in to curse the foreigners. No one would help with the building work and Mr. King had to be his own handyman, general laborer, carpenter, builder, contractor and foreman. But he stuck to his work and by April 1953 it was possible for Miss McCoughtry and Miss Longmire, a nurse, to join Mr. and Mrs. King. The King's contributions to the Kullo church cannot easily be estimated. They spent more than thirteen years there, often cut off from the outside by the rains and swollen rivers, until the Missionary Aviation Fellowship came in. It was Mr. King who arranged for a nearby hilltop spine to be leveled so that it could accommodate the single-engine aircraft of MAF. Even so, the aircraft lands into a hillside and takes off into a valley, spending the half-hour or so of the flight to Jimma twisting up and down the precipitous valleys with its wings nearly scraping the mountaintops. It was Mr. King, too, who channeled a stream from higher up the mountain into the mission compound so that the missionaries could grow their own vegetables.

The churches grew. At first the Buri church, founded by Kullo families who had taken refuge in Wallamo in the days of the occupation, was quite unaware of the existence of other churches in Kullo. Four of their menfolk were arrested just after they had settled back into Kullo, but just at that time the Christians from the churches to their north, who had been arrested and sent to Jimma for trial, returned, having been acquitted, and the authorities decided not to press charges against the Buri men. The Buri church went from strength to strength until by 1955 they had given birth to three new churches, Fullasa, Hal'an and Shota.

The Wallamo evangelists frequently took Kullo wives and settled down to family life. This proved a great benefit in times of opposition, for a man who could claim relatives in Kullo could not easily be expelled from the area. Ato Tumebo Talla was one such evangelist, and he settled into Intalla. His wife's sister was living in nearby Samara. She was a Christian, but to the displeasure of the church, she had married an unbeliever. The church at Intalla made a practice of visiting her home in order to get the husband converted and to regularize the unusual situation. The visiting produced even more than the hoped for result: both her husband and a number of neighbors were converted and they began a church.

A little to the north of Kullo, but also on the west bank of the Omo river, is Janjero. There, at Gannita, was the first church. A young schoolboy, Tekle, heard the Wallamo evangelists at Gannita preaching and made his way to the mission down at Saja to find out more. Miss Dronen, who first went to Saja in 1949, talked with him and gave him some leaflets which, in his innocence, Tekle took back to school with him at Fofa. The headmaster burned the tracts and ordered the schoolboys to give their compatriot a beating. Bemused, Tekle went back to Saja, this time finding the two Wallamo evangelists there. Through the night they spent the hours explaining matters to him. He understood and became a Christian. This time he took a copy of John's gospel back to Fofa with him! His book was burned and he was expelled.

Undeterred, he continued meeting with the other Christians. His father disowned him. He was arrested. For six months after his release he attended the Bible school at Hosanna, run by the SIM and when he returned home he found ten Christians. A school was built and Tekle was appointed headmaster. Nearly two hundred children crowded in when the school opened at Gannita. Tekle was imprisoned again and again. It was January 1953 when the people finally burned the school down. The believers built it again and added a church. The story of the center pole of the church at Gannita is the story of the spirit of Janjero.

Near to Gannita was a sacred grove. The Gannita Christians decided that one of the trees in the sacred grove would make a fine center pole for their church. They approached the owner of the grove. Afraid actually to sell the tree, he merely agreed that *if* they were able to fell the tree they might pay him for it. As the Christians set about felling the tree, four men arrived with a calf to be sacrificed at the grove. Unperturbed, the Christians chopped on until the tree fell. That tree-trunk remains today the center pole of the church at Gannita.

In 1954 the Wallamo evangelists in Janjero were replaced by Kambattans, since the Kambattan language is related to Janjero. Ato Eha, a very forceful Kambattan evangelist, located at Jimma, was to oversee the arrangement. By 1955 there were three churches. Wolde-Senbet Kossaye went to the Gannita school, was converted and became a teacher. Then he moved on to Wargu where he opened a second school. A good number of older people were converted and with the school there was soon a church. The third church was formed through Ababa, who came from Gogawre, but met the two early converts Habte-Maryam and Haile-Maryam down at Saja, talked with them and with the missionaries, and went back to Gogawre a converted man. His family followed his lead and the church began.

But with the three churches in existence there came trouble. The three Kambattan evangelists returned to Kambatta to discuss the position in Janjero with the elders. They decided that the Janjero churches should form part of the Kambatta church. They would be subject to the direction of the Kambattan elders, meeting at Hosanna.

Independent to the core, the Janjero Christians refused to accept this. Ato Eha came hurrying across from Jimma to add his authority to that of the evangelists. But the Janjero church would not budge. The Kambattan evangelists left; Janjero believers replaced them: Geremu at Gannita, Wolde-Senbet at Wargu and Ababa at Gogawre. And at the same time a monthly Janjero council meeting was commenced to parallel the structure of the Kambatta church.

This was an unfortunate time for the Kambattan evangelists. They were also asked to leave Kullo, in favor of the Wallamo evangelists. Kullo bordered on Timbaro, in southern Kambatta, but also on Wallamo to the east. So evangelists had come in from both districts. Now, while the Wallamo and Kambatta churches agreed on most things, circumcision was a point on which they differed. As we have seen, right from the start of the work in Wallamo the converts had picked on circumcision as a fundamental of pagan Wallamo society. They completely forbade its practice by believers. In Kambatta, however, the rite had much less significance and had never been an issue. What about Kullo?

The Wallamo evangelists preached against circumcision. The Kambattans taught tolerance. In March 1955 the matter came to a head at the Bible conference held at the Intalla church. Ato Molisso, a leading Kullo elder, was circumcised. Others followed his example. The rest of the church demanded that these men be disciplined. Their advisers spoke with a divided voice. The conference chose to stay with the Wallamo position against circumcision. The Kambattans were advised to move to Janjero, although the Kullo Christians could not have realized that the door there would be shut to them, also.

Across in Darassa the church was growing rapidly. There had been just one church in 1949, at Gola, but by 1955 there were eighteen and the first church had been established in southern Darassa, not far from Yirga Chaffee. In this area conversion seemed to be the result of the movement of dispossessed Darassan believers who migrated southward where land was more readily available, rather than through evangelists. The church at Buko, some six hours on foot southeast of Yirga Chaffee, was formed through a believer from Dilla who settled there. His witness led to the conversion of his neighbors. The area is very fertile and the people relatively prosperous: the coffee grows practically without any attention at all and bananas flourish. Every man is a trader and the price of the coffee crop is at once transformed into something negotiable. Even the children will turn merchant: during the coffee-picking season they buy bread in the villages at wholesale price and then trek up into the hills to sell it to the hungry workers. Thus, when the price of Amharic Bibles was suddenly reduced by half the Darassa people quickly bought up stocks at the new price and hurried to sell them in areas where the news had not penetrated at the old price. The church in 1949 grew to eighteen churches by 1955 and five years later there were thirty-six. In 1957 the first church constitution for Darassa was drawn up and signed at Dilla by twenty-nine Darassan Christians and three missionaries: Mr. Brant, Mr. Jongeward and Mr. Lloyd Stinson.[4] (See Appendix B.)

The Sidamo work had reached down into Darassa country and the church was steadily extending its influence toward the SIM station at Burji. Across Lake Abbaya, the church had advanced from Wallamo to Chencha, and westward to Bulki but a depressing gap still existed between the Wallamo and the Burji work. Bako appeared to be the key to filling the gap.

The entire area to the south of Addis Ababa, but north of the Kenya border, is referred to by linguists as the "fragmentation belt," and the process of fragmentation is exemplified by Bako. At least twelve different languages are spoken by tribes living within easy reach of the town. Four of these have been effectively reached by the SIM from Bako: the Ara, Banna, Male and Dime. The Galeb and Mursi have contact with the American Presbyterian Mission to the west. The Hamer and Tsemai groups have been reached by SIM work at Hamer, opened by Mr. and Mrs. C. Bonk in 1969. The Bumi, Karro and Paydi tribes have scarcely been contacted at all.

In 1954 Mr. and Mrs. Don Gray, with Mr. Bill Carter, commenced work for the SIM at Bako. Most of the building supplies were brought in on the heads of carriers from Bulki, sixty miles away to the west. In April 1957, with the Kullo work well established, Ato Umboli moved to Bako with Ato Giradi. Shortly afterward the pair were joined by Ato Shanka who had been first in Sidamo and then in Bulki, to the west. Here the church and the mission were evidently reaching the limit of the linguistic and cultural pocket in which the church had grown to that time. By 1960 there was still no apparent sign of a breakthrough in Bako,

4. There has been no split in Darassa comparable to that which occurred in Kambatta-Hadya. Relationships between the Norwegian Lutheran Mission and the SIM and between the respective churches have been consistently good.

although eastward in Burji there were, by this time, thirty church-es.

At Bulki the growing church had established itself without the presence of the SIM. By 1950 there were two churches, established through the Wallamo evangelists Ato Israel and Ato Yohannes and, later, Ato Mahe. Yohannes, who got married just before moving into Bulki, was imprisoned because of his preaching at Kazza, and Ato Mahe was sent in by the Wallamo church with food for the imprisoned evangelist. He then stayed on at Baga, as evangelist. Baga became the second Bulki church. When Yohannes was released he at once returned to his preaching at Kazza. Ato Alemu, an Amhara who had heard Mr. Ohman preach before the Italian occupation, was very receptive and it was near his home at Kazza that the first Bulki church was established. Three more evangelists came in from Wallamo, Lalisa Tantu went to Kanchi, Ato Jara Bakalo to Uba and Ato Shanka to Goybe, where he found two more believers from Mr. Ohman's days in the area. By 1953 there were eight churches. When the SIM was able to move into Bulki again, in March 1959, there were forty churches and almost two thousand baptized church members.

One of Ato Mahe's converts was a man named Diko. When he became a Christian he was disowned by his tribe and lived as an outcast. For two years he traveled around with Ato Yosha of the church at Churamo; soon they numbered five believers, then there were eight households. Still they were ostracized by the tribe, hav-ing to live apart and even to find their own burial ground. But the fearlessness of the believers impressed the rest in spite of themselves. With some fear they spoke of "Diko's God."

The church was pecking at the constraining envelope which marked the limits of her advance. In Bako new tribes were being reached, and the southernmost boundaries passed. On the north-ern boundary, too, a movement was apparent. Ato Wolde Bela-chew, like so many other young Chabos, moved to Addis Ababa where he and his brother bought a shop. He also began to read. His reading material included a Bible, and he began to realize uneasily that what he had learned from the Orthodox church about Christianity did not seem to agree with what the Bible said about it. He returned to Chabo and began to discuss his problems with anyone who would listen. His criticism of the *Tezkar,* the memorial feast for the remembrance of the dead, was not very important, perhaps, for there had been a movement to restrict the lavish out-lay of money on these feasts. But his criticism of the adoration of Mary was a different matter. Of the collection of extra-biblical books venerated by the Orthodox church, he rejected the popular one called the "Miracles of Mary." He repeatedly quoted Gala-tians 1:8, "But though we, or an angel from heaven, preach any other gospel unto you than that which we have preached unto you, let him be accursed."

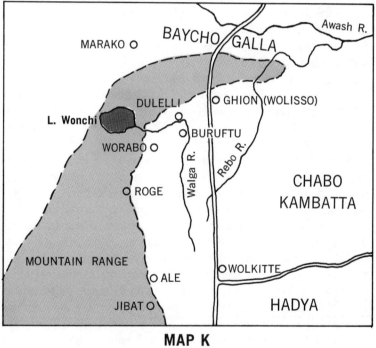

MAP K
THE CHABO CHURCHES

Wolde felt that the church needed reformation because it preached "another gospel." Memhir[5] Wolde-Meskel, Lemma Be-yenne and Ato Galata soon followed his lead, remaining within the Orthodox church mahabir, or fellowship, but viewed with

5. The title *Memhir* is given by the Orthodox church to its teachers. The word comes from a Ge'ez verb *mahare* (to teach).

suspicion by priests and people. In 1959 a woman who had
listened to many of the discussions and been intrigued by many
of the questions which were asked, went to Addis Ababa. She
spoke to Ato Gossaye Zemedhun, the evangelist employed by the
church associated with the SIM in Addis Ababa, and told him
that there were people in Chabo who needed Bible teaching. On
December 21, 1959 Gosaye paid his first visit to the Chabo people at Buruftu. See map K. As he was himself a former priest of
the Orthodox church he could be very specific in his teaching. He
preached at the funeral of the father of a man named Abdissa,
and from that time onward a number of the Chabo people began
to separate themselves from the mahabir. Gosaye remained that
first time for only two weeks, but in the early part of 1960 he
was frequently in Chabo.

The Darassa church, which had now become a missionary
church, sent Ato Gebeyehu to help the Chabo believers. Ato Yohannes and Ato Matewos were sent over by the Kambattan church
a little to their south.[6] Ato Gosaye baptized sixty in the first baptismal service.

At the end of another decade there were more than three hundred churches in Wallamo and over two hundred in Kambatta. In
Sidamo more than fifty congregations were meeting and thirty-
six churches were scattered through Darassa. Further down the
Rift Valley, at Burji there were forty churches where at the beginning of the ten years there was not one. Bako was only just
beginning to stir, but further to the west, at Bulki, there were
forty churches and the same number in Chencha. Across the Omo
river twelve churches were growing in Kullo and the independent-
minded Janjero church numbered four congregations. As Kambattans and Wallamos continued to spill across the Bilate river into
the Shashamane area, ten churches had sprung up. In the ten
years the number of churches had again doubled and now the
church was beginning to reach out beyond the area in which tribal
unity was an important factor, to the tribes which formed the
containing envelope.

6. The Darassans have proved to be the more effective evangelists. Contact with the Guji Galla in the Bilate Valley means that Darassans speak
the Galla language. Although Chabo Gallinya differs from the dialect
spoken by the Guji Galla, the Darassans soon picked it up.

15

The Role of Persecution

From its beginnings the young church in the south of Ethiopia has faced opposition which has often been violent. When the work in Wallamo began to grow, Ato Toro and Ato Gofato, evangelists in the Koisha area, were imprisoned. The church then established a pattern of conduct which has, in general, been followed ever since. In the main, food is not provided for prisoners in the provincial jails, so the churches provided for Toro and Gafato during their imprisonment. Frequently the food provided by the enthusiastic church was so abundant that many of the unconverted prisoners were fed too. This practical demonstration of Christian solidarity frequently brought about the conversion of other prisoners. In Kambatta, imprisoned Christians preached and sang in prison to such effect that the police hurriedly released them, commenting ruefully: "You're more trouble *in* prison than out of prison!"

When persecution hit the Sidamo church, several believers were in the Yirga Alem jail. A missionary on his way to the capital obtained permission to visit them. He felt fairly sure of gaining an interview with the Emperor in Addis Ababa and offered to speak for the prisoners, to get them released from prison. The believers replied in a surprising way. "When were we in prison?" they asked. "God brought us here and He will take us away again. There is no need to speak to the Emperor for us."

This policy of nonresistance has, in the main, proved effective. The churches simply outlast the opposition. They will speak out for themselves in court, but in general, they don't seek the intervention of higher authority. At times, however, the church has broken this principle.

In April of 1947 thirty new Kambattan believers were im-

147

prisoned. Even mission employees were not safe and Miss Mac-
Luckie had to ride into Hosanna to secure the release of the lad
who helped her in the house. The governor had the lad released,
and although he promised to assist the elders in the accusations
which were made against the Christians, still the persecution continued. In January 1948 one of the imprisoned believers died in
jail at Hosanna. Three days later forty-five believers were released
and after another four days all but two of the remainder were
freed.

The two detained were accused of murder. The accusation arose
in a curious manner. Police entered the home of a believer and
tied him up, then they suspended him from the roof of his house
by a rope tied around his chest. His screams brought neighbors
in and during the confusion that followed, several shots were fired.
A police sergeant later died from gunshot wounds. It was impossible to determine how the injuries were received, but eventually the man who had been hanging from the roof was accused of
the murder and sent to Assela to stand trial.

Eventually the church decided to send Ato Ababa Bushiro and
Ato Shigute to Addis Ababa to appeal to the Emperor for justice. As
we have seen, Ababa got the letter into the hand of the Emperor and
His Excellency Asrate Kassa, the governor-general, was ordered to
conduct an enquiry. He was in Hosanna from December 21 to 27,
1950 and discussed the situation with Dr. R. N. Thompson. Bob
Thompson has had a remarkable career. He influenced the beginnings of the Ethiopian educational system and even the affairs of
the embryo Ethiopian Air Force. He was later to become a Canadian Member of Parliament and a special emissary to Congo at
the time of the Simba troubles there.

The governor-general was anxious to hear the cases against
some of the prisoners. The police objected that it was impossible
to locate all the witnesses. One man was brought forward, accused
of building a church on someone else's land. He had been sentenced to twelve months in prison. But when his case was examined it was quickly shown that the land was, in fact, his own.
He was ordered to be released. The Hosanna governor quickly
freed a second man, similarly improperly imprisoned, but the
governor-general's visit was only a brief one, and nothing could
be done for the rest.

Asrate Kassa and Dr. Thompson discussed the situation and reached agreement on ways of ending friction. The mission schools were to be open to all and not to believers only; pastors and elders must refrain from taking part in politics. Freedom for preaching in Kambatta was guaranteed, except in the immediate vicinity of Orthodox churches or preaching directly to Orthodox church congregations. Churches could be built on any privately owned land. Believers might not be arrested on merely religious charges. Very important, it was agreed that church members should not be required to pay the annual tax to the Orthodox church, nor would they be required to assist in building Orthodox churches. The derogatory name "Protestant" was to be dropped. But Bob Thompson refused to agree to the proposal that the church elders should act as guarantors for the good conduct of the rest of the church.

In fact, the visit of the governor-general had little lasting effect: as usual, when the visible representatives of central government went away, the local authorities virtually ignored them and the persecution continued. The Hosanna governor had Shigute and Abba Gole arrested, and paraded them before a huge crowd. Sarcastically, the governor asked the people why they allowed illiterate men to lead them. He called on Shigute to read to them, anticipating that he would be unable to. Shigute quickly opened his Bible, turned to the last chapter of Mark's gospel and read aloud the verses which were heard over and over again in Kambatta, Wallamo, Sidamo, Gamo-Gofa: "He that believeth and is baptized shall be saved, but he that believeth not shall be damned" [Mk 16:16]. "Go ye into all the world, and preach the gospel" [Mk 16:15]. The first verse is the message they took; the second is their authority for taking it. Outraged, the governor next accused the two men of being drunk, at which Abba Gole laughed outright, recalling that the very same accusation was made against the apostles at Pentecost.

One of the more serious assaults on the church took place in Gamo province in February 1951. A little before this, twelve of the believers had been arrested, including Ato Gimbo. Three of them died in prison. After various terms in prison the rest were released, whereupon a great meeting of the church was held to give thanks for their preservation. Many more joined the church. More arrests followed and the believers were actually forbidden to supply the prisoners with food. Persecution turned to plundering, and eventually hundreds of homeless and terrified Christians fled for refuge to the SIM compound at Chencha. There they remained for more than a year. Eventually Ato Gimbo and Ato Petros, another elder, obtained evidence of the plundering and made their way secretly to Addis Ababa. When their story was confirmed, government action was swift. Fifty of the plunderers were arrested, and a total of some four thousand dollars was awarded to the church as compensation.

Actually the persecutors were more frightened by the almost total crop failure in the normally fertile Ocholo district than by the swiftness of the government action. Those who had squatted on the land of the refugees found themselves close to starvation, but with the return of the Christians matters swiftly stabilized.

The following year it seemed it was the turn of the Burji church to suffer. Even the missionaries were not immune. Mr. Fellows was confined to the mission compound under threat of imprisonment if he disobeyed. Defying the ban, he made his way to the provincial capital, Yirga Alem, and brought back a letter confirming his right to preach in Sidamo. Opposition continued, but failed to deter the converts; the first baptismal service in March 1953 was followed by a second and then a third, when fourteen were baptized at Dereba. Opposition sprang up on every hand. In sympathy, the church at Dilla sent sixteen dollars to help with the care of the prisoners. An Orthodox priest filed seven accusations against Mr. Fellows, although in court at Dilla he withdrew them all, admitting that his aim was simply to shut the mission station. He partially succeeded, for the governor had banned mission preaching until the case was settled. In 1954 a similar pattern of opposition developed in Wallamo and there, too, the missionaries were ordered not to leave the mission compound.

Still the period was one of accelerated growth. In August of 1954 fifty-one were baptized at a service in Damota, 243 in the Cherake district and over four hundred in Admancho. In November the believers poured into Otona for their annual Bible conference, addressed by Dr. Joe Church and Rev. William Nagenda from the revival area of Uganda.

Janjero continually faced clandestine opposition and arson from its early days. In 1958 it broke out afresh over the case of Abba Fita. Each year, in Janjero, it was the custom for a calf to be sacrificed to Atokamo, the spirit of a sacred mountain. Its blood was sprinkled on the ground and was supposed to gain respite from the spirits for a year. The calf was paid for by a levy on the people. Abba Fita refused to pay his share. He could not, of course, be dealt with criminally for this, but instead he was charged with a crime against the Orthodox church.

The accusation was that he had called the ark a "lump of wood." Now it is the ark of an Orthodox church which consecrates the church, and it is viewed with a respect amounting to superstitious dread by many uneducated people. Perhaps Abba Fita *had* called it a "lump of wood." At any rate the accusation was sufficient to ensure his imprisonment and he was sent to the Jimma prison for a year. Violent prejudices were aroused in Janjero, some of the believers began to waver, church attendance dropped off. After nine months, however, Fita was released as a mark of clemency on the Emperor's birthday. His safe return to Janjero, and his confident witness to the other Christians meant much to the waverers and the churches filled again.

The following year the Kambattan church was again under pressure, and in 1960 and 1961 it was the turn of Sidamo. In one Darassan church every literate member was arrested. In March 1960 the little group of reformers in Chabo faced the same phenomenon. The Darassan evangelists, Wolde and Lemma, were arrested, the two Kambattan evangelists were hounded from the district, and the homes of the Christians were attacked. Ato Lemma's home was burned down; the homes of Ato Leggese and Ato Gabre-Mikael were mobbed. The people from nine balabbat districts met together, and expressed their determination to wipe out this movement. It appears that the most likely cause of hot tempers in Chabo was the reformers' rejection of Mary as mediatrix. This clashed both with the Orthodox church doctrine, and with the pagan, female atete cult which also associated itself with Mary.

The believers were scattered; some took to the hills, some found refuge on the mission station at Wolisso, forty-eight made their way to Addis Ababa. Their arrival incidentally, coincided with the visit of Billy Graham to the capital, and the Chabo believers were taken aback by the thousands of other Christians asssembled at the football stadium.

Their complaint was heard, and Colonel Azaz of the security department was sent to Chabo to restore order. But as in Kambatta so it was when once he had returned to Addis Ababa matters returned to their earlier condition. As feeling in the district continued to run high, the governor called a meeting at which the believers were told that they would be dealt with conclusively. Some of the mob actually brought ropes with them for the hanging that they were certain would follow the assembly. But Abba Wolde-Tinsae was present and his advice strongly swayed the governor.

This man is known throughout Ethiopia for his miracles and healing powers. His compound at Wolisso is lined with bottles containing beetles and worms of many kinds said to have been extracted from the ears, noses and toes of those who came to him. There are great Bible texts fashioned from the thousands of beads which were cut off the necks of the qalichas who came to him for healing and there are impressive, meticulously kept ledgers detailing the names, illnesses, treatments and outcomes for the thousands who have consulted him. Although he is an Orthodox priest, he counselled restraint. He recognized that the reformers were true believers.

When the governor spoke to the assembly he followed the advice of Abba Wolde-Tinsae. He refused to become involved in discussing religious issues, but he insisted on the maintenance of law and order. He ordered the crowd to go off and make peace with one another. The people heard him in disbelief. "He himself has turned mission," they muttered. But from that point on, matters began to cool off and regular meetings were again commenced by the believers.

This widespread and continuing violent opposition to the church in the south is a prominent factor in the development of the church, in the sifting of the true from the false. No one was likely to join this group of believers from social motives. But what did lie behind it?

First of all, it must be stated categorically that this persecution was not a manifestation of government policy. As we have seen, whenever the facts came to the attention of the central government, vigorous action was initiated. But on the whole, the policy of the church was not to seek government intervention, at least until major crises arose. And the generally poor communications in the southlands meant that the administration of any area was essentially a matter for the local governor, and was only peripherally subject to the scrutiny of the central authorities. The Ethiopian constitution specifically guarantees freedom of worship to the people of the empire, but it has not proved easy to implement these provisions in the more remote areas.

The persecution has invariably originated from the hostility and suspicion of the Orthodox church. In the wake of the missionaries and the churches there always came education, not schools where the children learned only Ge'ez, which they could not understand, but where the language used was Amharic. The Bible became an open book. The hold which the thousands of often ill-educated priests had had on the people began to loosen. Tragically, instead of recognizing the immediate need for reform, the Orthodox church persecuted the new Christians. Rather than cleaning their old and tarnished lamps, they determined to extinguish the light of the new. Predictably they failed.

"The Bible became an open book."

But the persecution and the suspicion had another focal point: the foreign missionary. There is a deep-rooted suspicion of the foreigner which can be traced, at least in part, to the intrigues of the Jesuit missionaries of the seventeenth century. They encompassed the submission to Rome of Emperor Susenyos, and precipitated civil war. Susenyos was forced to abdicate and his son, Fasilidas, expelled the missionaries. Even the nearness of a missionary to the Emperor, such as Lambie to Ras Tafari, must have caused some disquiet.

With improved communications and with the measure of enlightenment that education has brought, the cruder forms of persecution are dying out. It is much to be regretted that the World Council of Churches declined to take action in the conflict in Ethiopia, for the Orthodox church is a member of the council. Paul Verghese prepared a very fully documented report on the persecution for the WCC, but no action was taken.[1] The young church has outstayed its opponents. And it could be that with the declining status of the foreign missionary and a decline in the politcial influence of the Orthodox church, persecution from this source might end.

1. The author presented this matter to a former vice-president of the World Council of Churches who admitted the existence of the report on Ethiopia but intimated that they could do nothing to help. They had "no authority" to deal with the conduct of a member church. The author has not himself seen the report.

16

1960-1970

Between 1950 and 1960 the number of churches in the south of Ethiopia had doubled from fewer than four hundred to some eight hundred. In the succeeding ten years the numbers again doubled. But with the exception of a quiet movement among the Alaba peoples, initiated principally through Mr. Glen Cain, his second wife, and daughter Naomi, there was little movement beyond the boundaries we have already encountered.

In September of 1961 Mr. and Mrs. Alex Fellows moved to Bako. A week after their arrival Mr. Fellows was out at Bassi when Addisu, the first convert in the area, undertook to follow Christ. In January of the following year Ato Maja came from Wallamo: he had worked with Mr. Fellows in Burji earlier and knew his ways. Maja took Addisu along as his interpreter and began an extensive preaching tour. Thirteen conversions resulted and on May 24, 1962 there followed the first baptismal service in Bako.

The women's work grew, too, under the influence of Mrs. Fellows. Fifty-three women attended the first women's conference in May 1963; five years later there were five hundred. Mr. Fellows set an example he expected the Wallamo evangelists to follow by continually being out among the people. The Koybe church, among the Male people, owes its origin to the visit of Mr. Fellows to the village: Ato Gircha, his brothers and his father all believed together, one of the comparatively rare cases from southern Ethiopia of group conversion. Today there are more than one hundred members of the Koybe church, and eight more churches have sprung into existence through their preaching.

Incidentally, some of the converts had a shock introduction to the implications of their new faith. Addisu was preaching beside the trail when four men were converted. Just at that point a man stopped and demanded to know why he was preaching. Most of the non-Amhara people of this district were accustomed to being required to give an answer for their conduct to any official who cared to ask, so Addisu explained. Their interrogator tied Addisu's hands behind his back and made him carry a bundle of butter by a string clenched between his teeth. He then loaded a sack of barley onto his back. The four new converts were likewise loaded up and driven into the town like a train of donkeys. This was Addisu's second run-in with authority and he took the ensuing imprisonment calmly. But it must be almost unique to be thrown into prison only minutes after being converted, as were the four.

But as elsewhere, opposition merely encouraged the church. By the end of 1965 there were thirty-two churches and by 1970 there were forty-four making a total of more than fifteen hundred members.

In Sidamo there was a lull in the outreach of the church from 1958 until 1962. For a good part of this time the missionaries were not allowed to visit the churches although the authorities interpreted this rule with varying measures of strictness. The church appeared quiescent. But in 1962 the work took off again: reports began to come in of new churches being formed and of large numbers being baptized. From Gunde church alone twenty-two new churches were established. See map L. By 1964 there were more than one hundred churches in the area. Then as later in Wallamo, dissatisfaction over the leadership of the church began to be expressed. Offerings dropped off, a general air of apathy fell on the believers. In May 1965 Don Gray, the missionary in charge at Wando, advised the church to hold new elections for elders throughout Sidamo. On July 16 there was a large gathering at the mission station; next day the meeting broke up as six of the main elders agreed to accept the discipline of the church. Two days later the new elections were complete.

Once again the church advanced. By 1969 there were four areas, Gata with forty churches, Yenasse with fifty-seven churches, Homatcho with forty-five and Chuko with forty-nine.

The work at Wando demonstrates the importance of stability

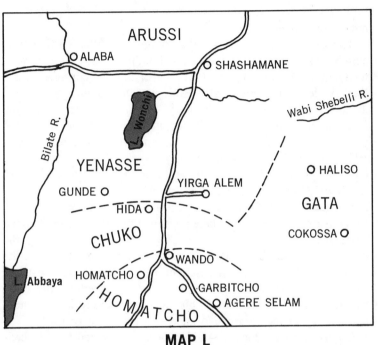

MAP L
THE SIDAMO CHURCHES

in missionary staffing. In 1963 Mr. and Mrs. Klassen came to Wando. Up to this point the Bible school at Wando had attracted but few students. The facilities offered compared poorly with the new elementary and training school buildings at the other end of the compound and Bible school staff had been changed so often. The Klassens remained. The enrollment grew so that a new building became imperative. In 1970 a second new building had to be added. More than three hundred men enrolled in the Bible school in September 1970 and there were another thousand men studying out in the Bible schools started by the churches themselves.

Nor is Sidamo an isolated instance of the advantages of a stable staffing of mission stations. The Chabo work labored for years under the handicap of a constant breakdown of communication between church and mission as the missionaries were appointed and then moved. But the Colemans were appointed to Wolisso in July of 1962 and have been able to gain the affection of the Chabo believers and even the respect of many who had opposed the reform movement.

The story of the growth of the church in southern Ethiopia is closely linked with the names of Dr. Lambie, Glen Cain and Walter Ohman. All would reject the idea of any human agency, but they all devoted themselves to Ethiopia. Dr. Lambie, the human dynamo, the catalyst, the visionary, led the way. Mr. Cain, the quiet, authoritative leader, joint deputy field director during the years of the Italian invasion and occupation, field director from 1948 until 1957, is still, in 1973, at work in Sidamo. And Mr. Ohman, whose name will always be associated with Wallamo, succeeded Glen Cain as field director in 1957.

What a life the Ohmans shared: the hard honeymoon trek to Bulki back in 1931, the Italian occupation, the Sudan and the years among the Maban people. They were even shelled by the *Atlantis*. On March 23, 1941, 120 missionaries embarked on the *Zamzam* of the Egyptian merchant navy. Her captain watched gloomily: "Mark my words, chief," he grumbled to the chief engineer, "It's bad luck for a ship to have so many Bible punchers and sky pilots aboard. No good will come out of this!"

On April 16 the German raider, *Atlantis,* sighted the blacked-out *Zamzam*. It was four o'clock in the morning when she opened fire. The second salvo smashed the radio cabin. The passengers boarded lifeboats, some of which capsized, others, splinter-riddled, sank, leaving the passengers struggling in the water. Miraculously there were only three serious casualties. When the captain of the *Atlantis* realized there were so many Americans among the passengers, he feared a new *Lusitania* incident, so he treated everyone with special care. They remained on the *Atlantis* only one day and were then transferred to the supply ship, *Dresden*.

Captain Jäger of the *Dresden* landed them at St. Jean de Luz in occupied France and from there the British were taken into internment and the Americans were repatriated by way of Spain and Portugal. In Portugal the Ohmans were found by Dr. Hambrook, who only a few days before had been with Rev. and Mrs. Horn of the SIM's London Office. He was able to speed up their repatriation. But no sooner were the Ohmans back in America than they were looking for another ship to take them to the Sudan.

The years that the Ohmans spent as administrators in Addis Ababa were good years for the SIM. The path for Mr. Ohman, not himself an administrator by choice, was smoothed by an outstandingly good administrator whom he inherited from Mr. Cain, Howard Borlase. Mr. Borlase moved steadily across Africa through his career as a missionary, starting in West Africa in 1936, and moving on to the Sudan, then to Ethiopia in 1948, when Glen Cain nominated him as his field secretary, and finally to Somalia as superintendent in 1967. During his years as Mr. Cain's field secretary he was also, effectively, deputy director. Glen Cain records briefly "He was a perfect second-in-command." Mr. Ohman was glad to have Mr. Borlase, who seemed to know everyone of any importance in Addis Ababa. The years flowed by, not without their difficulties, but with a remarkable measure of missionary harmony.

In 1966 Mr. Ohman retired from his appointment as field director. The next year he was back in Wallamo to face possibly the most trying period of his life. There was trouble in the church. No one could quite put his finger on the reasons, but the believers were uneasy. Support for the evangelists had dropped off. The number of men out as evangelists had dropped to forty and even those were not being supported properly. In some areas this reduction had been planned, in light of the new churches' increased ability to maintain themselves and to reach out with their own evangelists. But the general picture was one of discouragement and dissatisfaction. Mr. Ohman had one advantage over the men who had immediately preceded him as station heads at Soddu: he spoke the Wallamo language.

Church elders began to trickle into Otona to talk with Mr. Ohman. His advice was simple: do what the Sidamo church had been compelled to do only a few years earlier: elect new chief elders. Hundreds of men gathered in the large new Bible school building at Otona. To listen to them, to attempt to counsel the former elders, Manley Hodges, successor to Mr. Ohman as field director, was present. The church announced its intention to hold new elections throughout Wallamo. All the former elders would be required to stand down from the elections.

Some of the believers were indignant over attempts which had been made to have Mr. Ohman removed from the district. One elder stood up to address the gathering. "It has been said that Mr. and Mrs. Ohman have no children. But they *do* have children. We, the Christians of Wallamo, are their children."

The SIM was asked to supervise the elections. Mr. Ohman was ill so the Otona Bible School director was appointed as supervisor. He and Mr. Malcolm Hunter traveled by Land Rover and mule, on foot, over the miles of Wallamo to visit every district. Election procedure was simple. The supervisors assigned to each candidate a symbol: an ox, a Land Rover, a house. The symbols were explained to the Christians. Then the symbol was placed next to the candidate's upturned hat. As the believers filed into the church each was given two slips of paper, one to be placed in the hat of each of the two elders for whom the believer wished to vote. Electioneering did not always go smoothly: at one church a former elder, banned by his church from taking part in the election, hung his head through the window of the church, hurling abuse at the team of supervisors!

Afterward the supervisors, who always included at least three trustworthy elders from a different district, counted the votes and then went out to announce the result to the people. The elected elders then came forward, knelt in front of the whole body of believers while the supervisors placed their hands on their heads, one by one, and prayed for their future ministry. Invariably, a feast followed.

As confidence returned to the church, money again began to flow in for the evangelists. During the rainy season of 1969 the Bible school men were sent out in pairs as evangelists. For three months they traveled through the south. On their return they reported more than nine thousand conversions and the establishment of twenty-six new churches. All the expenses for this, extraordinary outreach were borne by the Wallamo church.

The life of the churches, whether in Wallamo, Kambatta, Sidamo or Gamo-Gofa, is simple. None of the churches use any musical instrument. Rarely is a hymn book evident, and this is only partly because of the high rate of illiteracy. They use their own antiphonal hymns which parallel the songs used out in the fields when men work together in plowing or harvesting. The hymn may be of any length. In the early days hymns tended to be almost interminable. Dana Maja, the converted slave owner from Wallamo,

Singing in church

did not appreciate such verbosity. One day he brought such a
song to an abrupt close when he interjected, following the tune
and rhythm of the song: *Marana, marana-o,* "For ever, for ever?"
Since then this has become the standard ending for the songs, and
church elders regularly use the phrase to indicate to the song
leader that he has gone on quite long enough.

The churches have no benches or pews, but on Saturday the
building is carefully swept out and freshly cut grass is spread on
the floor. Women and children sit on one side, men on the other.
There may be a single bench, or a few three-legged stools for the
elders or the preacher.

The Amharic Bible is used. Mr. Ohman had translated part of
the Bible into the Wallamo language before the occupation, and
Mr. Duff and Mrs. Couser had done the same for Hadya and had
the Scriptures printed by the Bible Society. It has been the official policy, however, to restrict printing to Amharic (although
both the Galla Bible and the Tigre Bible are permitted).[1]

1. More recently the United Presbyterian Mission has produced a New
Testament in the Anuak language. The Red Sea Mission team has begun
work on the Afar language, and the SIM has developed a Wallamo translation program.

In the early days the Bible tended to be taken very literally. When the missionaries returned to Wallamo in 1945 they found that the Christians had disposed of their goats under the influence of Matthew 25. They concluded that if the goats were to be sent to eternal fire, a Christian should obviously have nothing to do with them. The believers were also horrified to see the missionaries allowing dogs in their homes. Did not the Bible say "Beware of dogs?"

During a visit to Ethiopia Mr. Beacham was upset to discover that some believers still drank *talla,* the home-brewed beer, and even *aroqe,* the potent whisky. The missionaries explained that the church could not be bullied into legislating against drink. Not until a fight broke out between a couple of drunken Christians did the church realize the need for action. Now all members are expected to be teetotalers.

Observation of the missionaries' conduct had led to some other interesting rules. On Sunday it was permitted to pick fruit or vegetables that grew above the ground, but not to dig up anything that grew in the ground. Many churches had roses around them grown from cuttings taken from missionaries' gardens.

The district elders in Wallamo were called table elders, and their council was named the table or *terepeza.*[2] They met once each month. Apparently they had noticed that the missionaries never held any formal discussion unless they sat around a table and so they deduced that this must be the proper way to transact business. Communion is taken once a month, on a date decided by the table in each area. Honey water may be used; fermented wine is never employed. Their own unleavened bread, or *injera,* may be used, but in some areas ordinary bread has more recently been introduced.

Not all churches have a pastor, Kambatta being until recently a notable example of a church fellowship without pastors. But following Ato Abba Gole's visit to America in 1965 he advised the Kambattan churches that the appointment of pastors could strengthen the churches. The pastor, however, is by no means a president, as is often the case in the West. If he is not himself an elder, then he is subject to the elders. In several areas it is a rule

2. One of many Greek words which have found their way into Amharic.

that a man may not be a pastor unless he has attended one of the twenty-five SIM Bible schools.

The great annual event is the conference. This may last for four days and will, in Wallamo or Kambatta, be attended by as many as five thousand believers. The audience may change completely in the middle of the conference as half the family, having attended the first part of the conference, treks home to enable the other half of the family to attend the second half. They sleep mostly out in the open, for it is impossible to find accommodation for so many. The offerings are for the evangelists, and usually include clothing, taken off right there at the meeting. Nor is it uncommon to find livestock tied to the platform. Goats are frequent gifts, but even chickens are brought along. Larger animals such as mules may even be offered for the use of the evangelists. Such a gift is a real sacrifice, for a good mule may be worth sixty dollars.

Of formal organization there is very little. The churches are grouped into districts and the districts are organized into areas

Offerings for the evangelists at the annual conference

served by the table. The areas meet together once a year for the *andinnet,* a fellowship of all the related churches. They have a president and a secretary but the function of the group is solely fellowship, they have no power over the churches. Of formal clothing there is as little evidence. The clerical collar has never made its appearance and there is no distinctive dress or symbol of office for any of the church leaders. Nor are the church buildings particularly noteworthy: usually they are merely larger versions of the thatched houses in which the people normally live, although in the 1960's corrugated iron roofs have appeared.

Their educational program has advanced at an extraordinary rate and in April of 1970 there were 363 schools with nearly thirty thousand children enrolled in them, in addition to the sixty-four Bible schools they had established. More than a hundred full-time evangelists were serving away from their own areas. These schools, Bible schools, evangelists, and churches were all financed entirely by the church. By the end of 1972 there were more than two thousand churches in the fellowship.

In the story of the rise of this great church in southern Ethiopia the SIM has acted primarily as a catalyst, pointing the way to what might be done, training the Christians for their tasks, but functioning almost always as advisers, not as masters. There is no sense in which the church has been given its independence; it has always been independent.

In district after district some patently human, fallible missionary has been used to initiate a work, but the Spirit, acting in the awakened lives of the Ethiopians, has swept the movement along. Ohman in Wallamo, Duff and Couser in Kambatta, Cain in Sidamo and more recently Fellows in Gamo-Gofa and Brant in Darassa, the guiding genius of Lambie: all have played their part and made lasting contributions.

But the story of the church is not the history of the mission. It is rather the story of the hundreds of Ethiopian people, many of whom suffered a misguided persecution, but who, having found freedom from a devil-ridden world took the liberating news to the rest. It is to them: to Abba Gole and Shigute, to Dana Maja and Godana, to Daka and Tekle, to Jubato the stone counter, and to the many others whom I count as friends, that I must dedicate this book.

17

Retrospect

It would be good to leave the story of the church of southern Ethiopia there, but one last question must be asked and, if possible, answered. Why did it all happen? The immediate answer is simple: a sovereign God willed it to be so. None of us would quarrel with this answer, and yet the sovereignty of God does not operate in a vacuum; there always remains an area of human involvement. This area is open to our investigation as the sovereignty of God is not. This final chapter is concerned with the sphere of human involvement.

The strength of the church today, like the strength of a rope, lies in its individual strands. The individual strands of the church are perhaps indecisive, but woven together, they are vastly strong. There are three strands. First there is the cultural situation in which the church was cradled. Second are the uncompromising indigenous principles of the missionaries involved. And the third element is the strategic removal of the missionaries at the instant of the birth of the church. We shall look at each strand individually.

The missionaries did not select their proposed mission field. It was chosen for them. The founders of SIM work in Ethiopia had a plan, and Dr. Lambie made it clear that their aim was to advance from Addis Ababa southward to Lake Rudolph country and the Somalilands. Jimma was to be the halfway base for operations. But the discussions with the Orthodox church leaders, annoying at the time, delayed their departure from the capital until the rainy season was upon them. The rains forbade their crossing westward to Jimma, making the great Omo gorge impassable. But in confirmation of God's intervention was the totally unexpected appearance of the three governors from southwest Ethiopia in strategic positions in Kambatta, Wallamo and Sidamo, all three friendly toward Lambie and his mission. But this, in turn, links up with the remarkable linguistic situation in the area governed by the three. Kambatta, Wallamo, and Sidamo provided strategic centers for two extensive language families, covering a total area of between twenty thousand and thirty thousand square miles. Within this vast area, preachers could move and, without undue difficulty, overcome language barriers to make the good news clear.

It is, of course, pointless to ask what would have happened if the missionaries had proceeded with their original plan of a base at Jimma to service work on the southern border of Ethiopia. The SIM did not realize this original plan, and it was left for the United Presbyterian Mission to evangelize the southwest. Nor is it legitimate to assume that the SIM would have reaped a quarter of a century ago, what the Presbyterians are now reaping. We cannot know what might have been. But the appearance of Dejazmatch Mosheshe at Hosanna, Dejazmatch Yigezu at Soddu, and, dramatically, of Dejazmatch Biru at Agere Selam, when all three had been Lambie's friends years earlier and hundreds of miles to the west, makes it excitingly clear that the history books need to be re-written. They are concerned with the passing of kings and the chronicling of battles. And yet, while the history books dutifully record the life stories of kings and the battles they fought, the really vital factors are not written down at all. The stories of the Caesars are all there, but Jesus of Nazareth is not considered worthy of mention. And if later generations were to attempt to explain the world they know from the history books they have, they would find vast movements and changes in nations and peoples inexplicable. Southern Ethiopia, once the provenance of a great Moslem empire, later the home of pagan animists, is today transformed into a largely Christian community. A sovereign God prepared a cohesive society and set His appointees to rule it. And then He brought the missionaries to it.

Second we recognize the vital importance of the indigenous principles of the early SIM missionaries. The virile life of the church can only be comprehended when it is shared. There are no soaring church steeples and chimes of bells, no uncomfortable pews, no hymnals or organs, no vestments, no liturgy. The pastor, if there is one, is dressed like everyone else and enjoys no special privileges.

Perhaps there are some missionaries and some Ethiopians who regret that these things do not exist. Fine buildings, dignified preachers, impressive ceremonies are not to be found. Again it is true that the policy pursued by the mission, almost without exception from the beginning, of not paying for church buildings and not employing salaried preachers is misunderstood by many and, perhaps, even resented by a few. But the meeting of the SIM's field council in Soddu on December 1, 1933, at which the implications of indigenous principles were made specific for the work, marks a decisive and determinative point in the history of the church. Indeed, this is the pivot, on which much of what followed revolved. The vital passage from the minutes of that council meeting, unexciting as a corned beef sandwich, yet has a peal of bells, a sound of trumpets in it:

> The matter of having church buildings conforming to indigenous church principles was discussed, the immediate cause of this discussion being the commencement of such a building at Soddu, using some school funds from native sources. It was felt that this was not the right method, but that churches should be built by believers themselves and used for the purpose of houses of worship, and money expended should not be mixed with school money or other funds. That the missionaries might help, but it was not thought best that they provide the money or even a great part of it, but rather that it come from the believers themselves. It was directed that we inform the believers at Wallamo of our opinions and beliefs, in the hope that they would go on themselves in confidence and dependence on God, and complete the erection of this building, the foundations of which have already been laid, and that in the future we seek to conform more strictly to these principles of indigenous church building which we so earnestly believe in.

Who raised the matter? How did the missionaries at Soddu react to this implied criticism of their work? How did the believers themselves receive the news? We do not have answers to all these questions. However, twenty-seven missionaries, at Soddu for a spiritual life conference running concurrently with the council meetings, assembled to listen to the reading of the minutes. They

approved them unanimously. Let it be said again: this one paragraph, making explicit indigenous principles, was the pivot on
which great issues depended.

The third factor was the expulsion of the missionaries by the
Italians. It is no longer necessary to maintain the pretense that the
missionaries were not expelled. Recent, very limited access to the
archives at Rome makes it perfectly clear that expulsion was
the removal of the missionaries was needed before it could be
seen that the first converts had new life in Christ and were not
merely making conversion a prudent insurance policy for their
jobs. It is no quirk of inverted pride to say that the removal of
the missionaries at this formative period of the life of the church
was the best thing that could have happened.

It is, of course, immensely humbling to realize that what was
considered the midnight hour by missionaries, demanding the ral-
lying of prayer support from the thousands at the Keswick con-
vention in England, and the united intercession of the people of
God everywhere, proved, in fact, to be the dawning of a new day.
Staff and students at the Bible College of Wales spent long hours
travailing in prayer that the threat to Ethiopia might be removed.
Rees Howells, the principal, felt a great burden for the young
church in southern Ethiopia.[1] To them all it was inexplicable that
their prayers went not merely unheeded, but actually denied.

But with the missionaries scattered, some in the homelands,
some in the Sudan, the church grew explosively. The missionaries
were needed as heralds of God in the early years; they would be
needed again as Bible teachers in the years of consolidation that
lay ahead. But in the meantime, the burgeoning church developed
its own traditions of worship, made its own mistakes, and pio-
neered its own outreach.

The pattern of the growth of the church in southern Ethiopia,
for all its compact explosiveness, was not, in general, that of a
people's movement. The towns of southern Ethiopia are inhabited
mainly by the Amhara administrators, while out on the hills and
in the valleys live the local people, each with his patch of land,
his few cattle, his coffee trees, and each within calling distance of
his neighbor. The people live their individualistic lives. Brian

1. See Norman Grubb's *Rees Howells, Intercessor.*

Fargher's investigation in Darassa showed that the first fifty believers in fifty churches all stood for Christ as individuals, facing conflict with brothers and sisters, with mothers and fathers, with tribal elders and witch doctors. A husband would accept the new faith even though his wife rejected it or a young man might join the church while his parents remained outside. In Kambatta many of the early converts were interrelated, but even there conversion was a matter for the individual rather than for family, clan or tribe. This is not to deny that many a man would put off making his stand for Christ until he could return to the church, clinic or mission station with his wife so that they could "believe together." However, this was not the overall pattern. Energetically individualistic people rejected polytheism and custom, swelling their numbers until society itself was transformed.

Here in these three strands—the cultural situation in the south, the indigenous principles of the missionaries, the isolation of the church in the formative years—we have the strength of the church. In the present debates on the life of the church these factors demand the most careful study. They do not promise a magic formula which will somehow bend God's sovereignty to man's desires. But these are principles which a sovereign God has used once. And out of midnight a church was born.

Appendix A
Statistical Summaries

The figures quoted have been obtained from primary sources and not merely from station reports. They therefore differ slightly from some summaries issued by the SIM. An attempt has been made to discover the date on which each church was founded and thus to calculate annual totals.

TABLE 3
SIM-RELATED CHURCHES IN ETHIOPIA
(See map E.)

Year	1942	1945	1950	1955	1960	1965	1970
Wallamo	80	150	200	250	334	340	493
Kambatta	70	100	145	170	216	312	330
Sidamo(Wando)	0	0	3	26	56	139	191
Darassa(Dilla and Yirga Chaffee)	0	0	1	18	36	94	158
Burji	0	0	0	1	40	81	85
Gamo(Chencha)	0	0	5	30	42	75	100
Gofa(Bulki)	0	0	2	20	40	67	123
Bako	0	0	0	0	1	24	44
Kullo(Waka)	0	0	8	10	12	20	28
Janjero(Saja)	0	0	0	0	4	7	9
Arussi(Shashamane)	0	0	2	8	10	12	25
Chabo(Wolisso)	0	0	0	0	1	3	5
Other	0	0	3	5	8	10	12
Totals	150	250	369	538	800	1184	1603

CHURCH MEMBERSHIP

The churches do not keep rolls of church members, nor, apart from generally sporadic reports in SIM station records, is any account maintained of baptisms. An exception is Wallamo, where a fairly consistent record of baptisms in the Wallamo area appears to have been maintained. However, there is no guarantee that the record is complete: almost certainly some baptismal services have been omitted from the record. By using Mr. Davison's 1945 estimate of one hundred and fifty churches and fifteen thousand baptized members as a base, we can calculate church membership (see table 4).

TABLE 4
CHURCH MEMBERSHIP IN WALLAMO

Year	Number of Churches	Cumulative Total of Baptized Members*	Average Church Membership
1945	150	15,000	100
1950	200	21,000	105
1955	250	32,000	132
1960	334	52,000	156
1965	340	66,000	194
1970	493	81,000	164

*The precise total is available for each of the five-year periods; but because they are not reliable, the approximation to the nearest thousand is employed for these estimates.

The above statistics assume, of course, that all those baptized remain in the churches and that there are no deletions from church rolls for any cause. If we assume empirically an expectation of life of fifty years and an average age of the convert of twenty years, over a period of twenty-five years we may estimate the membership wastage by death to be approximately thirty thousand.

This would then bring us to a total baptized church membership in Wallamo of some fifty thousand in 493 churches. It would appear that Mr. Davison's estimate of one hundred members per church in 1945 has been the norm in Wallamo for many years.

In April 1970 an SIM statistical summary claimed 563 churches in Wallamo with 85,450 members. Even allowing for the number of churches (490 in the Soddu area, thirty in Kucha and forty-three in Bolosso), it is unlikely that average church membership could be as high as one hundred and fifty, particularly as two hundred of the churches have been formed in the period 1965-1970. The total baptized church membership should probably be, even on the basis of the larger total of churches, between fifty thousand and fifty-five thousand.

This would then suggest that the overall total baptized church membership, given in the SIM summary as 181,469, should be revised to a more realistic figure of 150,000.

AREA DEVELOPMENT

In Wallamo the growth of the church has remained fairly constant through the years. This is the only area for which we have records of baptisms kept with some consistency for a long period

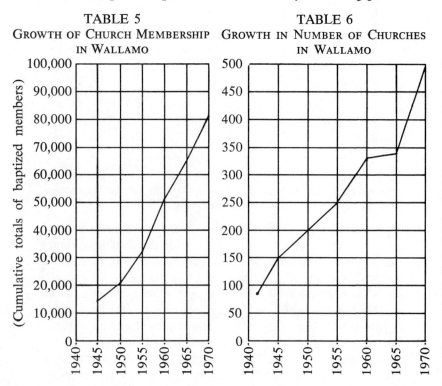

TABLE 5

GROWTH OF CHURCH MEMBERSHIP IN WALLAMO

TABLE 6

GROWTH IN NUMBER OF CHURCHES IN WALLAMO

of time. It is, therefore, possible to compare the rate of the establishment of churches (from table 3) with the rate of increase in the cumulative total of baptized members (from table 4). See tables 5 and 6. Again it is necessary to remember that the cumulative total of baptized members does not represent at the same time the actual total church membership, since allowance must be made for wastage.

The yearly rate of growth of the church[1] in Wallamo may be calculated with a measure of confidence from the SIM station register at Soddu. By comparing the numbers baptized in various years with the actual church membership in Wallamo, allowing for wastage through death and defection, a meaningful growth rate can be calculated (see table 7).

TABLE 7
WALLAMO CHURCH GROWTH

Year	Number of Baptisms	Total Baptized Membership*	Percentage of Growth
1960	4,232	33,400	12.7
1965	6,027	34,000	17.7
1969	7,422†	45,000	16.5

* Minus allowance for wastage.

† Actually 4,948 baptisms were reported in the first eight months.

It is almost certain that the figure of 340 churches (and thus some 34,000 church members in 1965), is incorrect; the Soddu register shows 388 churches at the beginning of 1966. We should therefore probably amend the growth rate of the Wallamo church for 1965 to some 15.8%. This then presents us with a slightly increasing rate of growth over the decade: 12.7% in 1960, 15.8% in 1965 and 16.5% in 1969.

1. A more detailed discussion appears in the author's article "An Indigenous Church in Southern Ethiopia" published in the *Bulletin of the Society for African Church History*.

In Sidamo the church exploded into life in the 1950s. Where in 1950 there had been four churches, there were more than four hundred by 1970 (see table 8).

TABLE 8
THE SIDAMO CHURCHES

	1950	1955	1960	1965	1970
Sidamo(Wando)	3	26	56	139	191
Darassa(Dilla)	1	17	28	74	89
Darassa(Yirga Chaffee)	0	1	8	20	69
Burji	0	1	40	81	85
	4	45	132	314	434

On the other side of Lake Abbaya, in Gamo-Gofa, a parallel movement was under way. In 1950 there were just seven churches, but twenty years later there were more than two hundred and fifty (see table 9).

TABLE 9
THE GAMO-GOFA CHURCHES

	1950	1955	1960	1965	1970
Gamo(Chencha)	5	30	42	75	100
Gofa(Bulki)	2	20	40	67	123
Bako	0	0	1	24	44
	7	50	83	166	267

PARALLEL MOVEMENTS

In southern Ethiopia the SIM-related churches cannot, generally, be compared with other churches, since other missions have not operated in the areas for comparable periods of time. Adventists and Roman Catholics have had a marginal representation in Kambatta, Wallamo and Sidamo, but only the Norwegian Lutheran Mission has committed itself to mission work in any way parallel to the SIM work. The figures in table 10 are taken from the NLM yearbook.

TABLE 10
NORWEGIAN LUTHERAN MISSION CHURCHES
IN SOUTHERN ETHIOPIA

	1950	1958	1960	1962	1964	1966
Number of Churches	2	29	39	76	172	184
Communicants	. . . .	1,729	2,494	3,755	6,217	9,313

These figures refer almost entirely to the Sidamo area, north of Dilla: NLM mission stations in the area include Yirga Alem, Agere Selam, Gata and Awassa. Further south they also have stations at Agere Maryam, Yavello, Negelli (Boran), Mega, Moyale, and others.

Appendix B
The Constitution of the
Darassa Church

The constitution which follows is the official translation of the document that was drawn up and signed at Dilla in 1957. No similar document exists for other areas.

*　　　*　　　*

ARTICLE I

The following are those recognized by the said organization:

1. Those from the Darassa and Gugee tribes who have trusted in Jesus Christ as their own personal Saviour, and who have produced the fruits of a born-again experience by obedience to the Word of God and to the church.

2. All of those authorized by the authorities of the Sudan Interior Mission are recognized as members.

3. Any true believers, regardless of tribe or church, coming with sufficient proof, in writing, of good Christian standing, agreeing to work with and to submit to the principles and practices of the said organization, may become members.

4. No-one who indulges in the use of intoxicating beverages or who uses tobacco in any form, will be permitted membership.

ARTICLE II

We desire it to be fully recognized that the Evangelical church of Darassa is founded upon the Word of God, recognizing the 66 canonical books as its only authority. Anyone who does not agree whole-heartedly with the principles of Scripture as laid down by the Organization will not be accepted into fellowship. False doctrine will not at any time be tolerated.

176

ARTICLE III

1. Any believer of good standing, after a year of probation, during which time there has been ample evidence of the new birth, and after he or she has been thoroughly examined regarding salvation, doctrine and the marriage state, may be permitted to be baptized by immersion.

2. All baptized members of the church who are not under discipline, and who have thoroughly examined their own hearts, may partake of the Lord's Supper.

3. Any matter regarding discipline from the Lord's Table,[1] either its being meted out or its cessation shall be revealed to the congregation before the emblems are administered.

ARTICLE IV

Any married person, whose marriage has not been sanctioned or approved by the main elders of the church will not be permitted baptism, communion or a position of authority in the church.

ARTICLE V

1. Any matter regarding marriage will be dealt with only by the main elders of the church who, considering the matter in the light of the Word of God, will give their decision.

2. The erection of a new church must have the approval of the main elders.

3. All teachers and preachers will be under their jurisdiction.

ARTICLE VI

The Darassa church does not recognize administration of the ordinances of baptism and communion, or any marriage, unless it has been performed by authorised persons, recognized by the church (any honourable marriage having taken place prior to faith in Christ is recognized). Any person violating these practices will be severely reprimanded or, if it be considered serious enough, he will be expelled from the church.

ARTICLE VII

1. If, within the area allotted to the SIM, there be no other church within reasonable walking distance, a group of five or more baptized believers desire to establish a new church, they

1. Church discipline usually involves being banned from communion for a set period of time.

may do so. The believers in that area may then, by their own choice and by secret ballot, appoint two baptized elders. If the believers are many, and if they so desire, they may add a third in like manner. If the growth of the work demands it two deacons may also be elected.

2. The work of the deacons will be as follows: They must work in agreement and in Christian love with the elders. They shall see that guests are cared for, that widows and the poor receive due consideration, and that the church is kept in good order. In areas where there are not enough members to establish a church, two deacons may be chosen to care for the local group. Deacons will be chosen in the same manner as the elders.

ARTICLE VIII

1. The election of elders and deacons will take place every two years, beginning from the month of *Tir* and the Ethiopian year 1949 (that is 1956-57).

2. All elections must take place in the presence of those appointed by the main elders.

3. The will of the Lord must be diligently sought, and the instruction of scripture followed.

ARTICLE IX

Until the growth of the church warrants a change, the following procedure will be followed; in agreement amongst themselves the elders and pastors of each church will send their representative in turn, for a period of three months, to the main elders' meetings. These elders, along with one or more representatives of the SIM, and any others selected by mutual agreement, will form the recognized body of main elders of the church. This body will convene every thirty days for prayer and counsel.

ARTICLE X

1. In local churches, where matters arise which do not affect the whole church, and do not require the forbidding of communion, the local elders have the authority to decide the matter.[2]

2. No matter will be brought to the main elders' meeting unless it has first been examined by the local church.

2. The Amharic word *guday* translated here as "matter" can also be rendered *dispute*.

ARTICLE XI

After each election all elected elders and pastors shall meet for the selection of a scribe.

ARTICLE XII

The money of the church shall be cared for by the scribe and one missionary. It is necessary that three elders be present each time the money box is opened to deposit or to withdraw money. The main elders will be responsible for the division of funds. The money pledged at the main conference will be used only for preachers and teachers.

ARTICLE XIII

The elders and chosen believers shall meet together at a chosen place or church once every thirty days. Matters of minor importance may be settled at these meetings if there is agreement. Any believer having a matter that has not been settled by his church, may bring the matter in writing to this gathering. If the matter cannot be settled there it may then be brought, in writing, to the main elders. Unless the said person be summoned, he or she may not appear in person at the main elders' meeting. The matter will be presented by an elder.

ARTICLE XIV

No matter of importance will be considered finalized unless agreement has been reached with the SIM.

ARTICLE XV

Once a year, two elders, with reasonable education and Bible training will be sent by the church to the meeting of the Evangelical Church of Ethiopia.

ARTICLE XVI

If the place of an elder or deacon, by reason of death, a change of location, or expulsion from the church, is left vacant, a replacement shall be made within two months. The election for replacement shall be done according to custom.

ARTICLE XVII

Any deacon or elder, pastor or evangelist or teacher, who does not carry out his duties in due order and proper manner, or without sufficient reason refuses to attend elders' meetings, may be removed from his office on the advice and consent of the main elders.

ARTICLE XVIII

After the election of the elders, all those with authority in the church, including the elders, pastors, evangelists and teachers, will meet together for a general assembly. At this meeting the Secretary and Treasurer will be appointed. Also it will be decided then as to the permission extended to other than regular elders to meet with the main elders. Any change in laws or practices may, upon agreement, be made at this meeting. All those attending will have an equal vote.

ARTICLE XIX

Regular pastors and teachers will be permitted to take part in all counselling. It is required that they take their turn in attending the main elders' meeting. In places where there are no elected elders or deacons, the preacher will represent the area.

Sources
Books and Articles

Bairu Tafla, Ato. "Four Ethiopian Biographies." *Journal of Ethiopian Studies* 7 (1969):2.

Barrett, David B. *Schism and Renewal. in Africa.* London: Oxford U., 1968.

Bingham, R. V. *Seven Sevens of Years and a Jubilee.* Toronto: SIM, 1942.

Buxton, David. *The Abyssinians.* London: Thames & Hudson, 1970.

Buxton, Edith. *Reluctant Missionary.* London: Lutterworth, 1968.

Cotterell, F. Peter. "An Indigenous Church in Southern Ethiopia." *Bulletin of the Society for African Church History,* 1971.

————. "Dr. Lambie: Some Biographical Notes." *Journal of Ethiopian Studies,* 1971.

Davis, Raymond. *Fire on the Mountains.* Grand Rapids: Zondervan, 1966.

Frank, Wolfgang, and Rogge, Bernhard. *The German Raider Atlantis.* Trans. R. O. B. Long. New York: Ballantine, 1956.

Forsberg, Malcolm. *Land Beyond the Nile.* Chicago: Moody, 1958.

Fuller, Harold. *Run While the Sun Is Hot,* New York: SIM, 1966.

Garratt, G. T. *Mussolini's Roman Empire.* London: Penguin, 1938.

Greenfield, Richard. *Ethiopia, a new Political History.* London: Pall Mall, 1965.

Grubb, Norman. *Alfred Buxton.* London: Lutterworth, 1942.

————. *C. T. Studd, Cricketer and Pioneer.* London: Lutterworth, 1945.

————. *Once Caught No Escape.* London: Lutterworth, 1969.

————. *Rees Howells, Intercessor.* London: Lutterworth, 1952.

Hooten, W. S., and Stafford-Wright, J. *The First Twenty-Five Years of the Bible Churchmen's Missionary Society.* London: BCMS, 1947.

Horn, L. W. *Hearth and Home in Ethiopia.* London: SIM, 1962.

Hunter, J. H. *A Flame of Fire.* Toronto: SIM, 1961.

Huntingford, G. W. B. *The Galla of Ethiopia.* London: International African Inst., 1955.

Lambie, T. A. *A Doctor's Great Commission.* Wheaton, Ill.: Van Kampen, 1954.

————. *A Bruised Reed.* New York: Loizeaux, 1952.

————. *Boot and Saddle in Africa.* New York: Revell, 1943.

Lambie, T. A., and Buxton, A. B. *Abyssinia.* New York: Abyssinian Frontiers Mission, n.d.

Martin, Ira D. *Ethiopia Calling.* London: Martin, n.d.

Maxwell, J. L. *Half a Century of Grace.* London: SUM, n.d.

Millham, W. T. T., ed. *East Africa.* London: Mildmay Movement, n.d.

Murphy, Charles. "Sinking of the *Zamzam.*" *Life* 10 (June 2, 1941): 34.

Neill, Stephen. *Christian Faith and Other Faiths.* London: Oxford U., 1970.

Petros, F. Tekle. "The Maskala." *Bulletin of the Ethnological Society* 2 (1961): 1

Playfair, Guy W. *Trials and Triumphs in Ethiopia.* Toronto: SIM, 1943.

Quinton, A. G. H. *Ethiopia and the Evangel.* London: Marshall, Morgan & Scott, 1949.

Ritchie-Rice, Esme. *Eclipse in Ethiopia.* London: Marshall, Morgan & Scott, n.d.

Ritchie-Rich, G., and Hooper, E. R. *Ethiopia.* London: SIM, 1933.

Roke, A. G. *An Indigenous Church in Action.* Auckland: SIM, 1938.

Sandved, A. *I Herrens Tjeneste.* Oslo: Norwegian Lutheran Mission, 1963.

Scott, Hugh. "Journey to the Gughe Highlands." *Proceedings of the Linnean Society of London* 2 (November 1952): 14.

Simpson, T. *Ethiopian Echoes.* London: SIM, n.d.

Steer, G. L. *Caesar in Abyssinia.* London: Hodder & Stoughton, 1936.

Tippett, Alan R. *Peoples of Southwest Ethiopia.* Pasadena, Calif.: William Carey Lib., 1970.

Trimingham, J. S. *Islam in Ethiopia.* London: Oxford U., 1952.

Ullendorff, E. *Ethiopia and the Bible.* London: Oxford U., 1969.

————. *The Ethiopians.* London: Oxford U., 1967.

Wilmott, H. *The Doors Were Opened.* London: SIM, 1960.

GENERAL MISSION PUBLICATIONS

Der Haster, yearbook of the Norwegian Lutheran Mission.

The Evangelical Christian, periodical from Toronto.

Intercom, internal information bulletin of SIM.

The Lightbearer, periodical published by SUM, London.

The Sudan Witness, periodical of SIM, London.

UNPUBLISHED DOCUMENTS

SIM MINUTES

Liverpool Council.
East Africa Field Council.
Conferences at Soddu: April 1930, June 1931, May 1932, April 1934.
Conference at Homatcho, April 1934.
Conference at Jimma, May 1934.

REPORTS

Missionary Prayer Meeting at Addis Ababa, April 16, 1931.
Clarence Duff on the death of Hoshe, February 9, 1931.
"A Notable Victory in Sidamo" by Dr. Hooper on the first baptism in Homatcho, December 25, 1932.
"A Moment I'll Never Forget" by J. H. Starling of his encounter with shiftas, 1936.
"Notes on the Situation in Wallamo" by L. A. Davison, May 1945.
Regarding Sheikh Zacharias by Dr. T. A. Lambie to Mr. E. E. Grimshaw.

EXTRACTS

From the Italian Archives in Rome, information dealing with the period of Italian invasion and occupation. I am deeply indebted to Mrs. Lass Westphal for her kindness in allowing me to see these abstracts, particularly those taken from the file on the SIM. *Ministero per l'Africa Italiana.* El. 3, Cart. 74, fasc. 205, subfasc. SIM 1936-38.

DIARIES

John Phillips' diary account of his days as a refugee in Kambatta, 1936.
Personal diaries of Syvilla Horn (née Ferron) and Rev. Eric Horn.
Dr. Lambie's diary account of his trip to meet Dr. Bingham, 1930.
Rev. G. Rhoad's diary account of the trip to meet Dr. Bingham, 1930.

MISCELLANEOUS

STATION DIARY

Station diary of SIM headquarters at Addis Ababa.

SIM STATION REGISTERS

Bako, Bulki, Burji, Chencha, Dilla, Durami, Hosanna, Jimma, Saja, Shashamane, Soddu, Waka, Wando, Wolisso.

LETTERS

Prayer letters circulated by Dr. Bingham 1927-1938.

Extracts from Mrs. Horn's letters to her mother, 1929-1931.

Letter from Miss Marion Walker to Miss Ferron regarding the first baptism at Homatcho, December 25, 1932.

INTERVIEWS

SIM MISSIONARIES

Miss Selma Bergsten

Mr. Glen Cain

Dr. Don Davies

Rev. Clarence Duff

Rev. Eric Horn

Mrs. Syvilla Horn (née Ferron)

Rev. Walter Ohman

Mrs. Marcella Ohman (née Scholl)

Rev. T. Simpson

Mrs. Olevea Simpson (née Sealey)

Rev. N. Simponis

EARLY CONVERTS AND CHURCH LEADERS

Gamo-Gofa area

Ato Addisu Jimma

Ato Ban'a Bonke

Ato Gimbo Sagamo

Ato Gofilo Gollo

Ato Gircha Sime

Ato Hadero Alala

Ato Jubato Ildimo

Ato Maya Baysu

Ato Tema Bashe

Kaffa area

Ato Degu Gabre-Maryam

Abba Goro

Abba Godu (husband of the first convert)

Woyzero Ha'da Shifa

Ato Tekle Wolde-Giyorgis

Ato Disassa

Ato Lemma

Kambatta area

Abba Gole
Ato Sabbaro Wossoro
Ato Ababa Bushiro
Ato Shigute
Ato Bekkele
Ato Bachore Katisso

Sidamo area

Ato Daka Sera
Ato Giyorgis Tajjima
Ato Ganame Unde

Wallamo area

Ato Aldada
Dana Maja
Ato Godana
Ato Tumebo Tella
Ato Toramo Leeka
Ato Markina Maja
Ato Wandaro

Index